Dedication

For my wife and kids.

The Hardest Job I've Ever Had
Stay-at-Home Dad

By: LA Gilbert

Published by LA Gilbert
Email: lancea.gilbert@hotmail.com
Cover Idea: LA Gilbert

First Edition
© *Copyright LA Gilbert 2019*

This book is copyright. Except for the purpose of fair review, no part may be stored or transmitted in any form or by any means, electronic or mechanical, including recording or storage in any information retrieval system, without permission in writing from the publisher. No reproduction may be made, whether by photocopying or by any other means, unless a license has been obtained from the publisher or its agent.

Contents

Preface	i
Introduction	ix
The Nanny-Go-Round	15
Morning Shift	23
Free Time (Not!)	35
The Witching Hour	47
Evening Shift (or, go the Fu*k to Sleep!)	61
Weekends and School Vacation	69
Relationships After Kids	83
Relationships After Kids (Part 2)	85
Isolation and Sense of Identity	93
Discipline and Guilt	103
Parent Twitter	119
The Best Job I've Ever Had	129
Hacks, Tips, etc.	137

Preface

"If you're so stressed at home with the kids, then go back to work!"

This is what I hear each and every time I try to 'express myself' when my wife arrives home from her job. Some might call it complaining, but after three kids have driven me to the brink of insanity and I haven't had the chance to interact with any adults in the past twelve hours, I'm compelled to express myself. Ok; it's complaining but at least I'm trying to make it seem more constructive.

I'm a stay-at-home dad. At the time of this writing, I've been at it for a year and the positive outcomes I expected have certainly come to fruition. My relationship with my thirteen-year-old stepdaughter has improved considerably and our four and five-year-old daughters (17 months apart) are now my little buddies. I'm bonding with our kids at a very critical juncture in their development, so the time I am investing in them now is invaluable. However, this is BY FAR, the hardest job I've ever had! It is an emotional and physical wrecking ball!

I had no idea, not even close, how brutally exhausting this job would be. And it's definitely a job. I don't know where the caricature of the stay-at-home parent as a robe-wearing dilly-dallier came from, but I'm insulted by it. Sorry; office jobs are EASY compared to this. In fact, any job where you deal with adults all day long is a cakewalk in relation to kid wrangling.

Since day one, I've been trying to convey to my wife just how hectic things are at home, but she's still adamant that I've got 'free time'! This leads me to believe that the life of a SAHP (stay-at-home parent) is an alternate universe that must be inhabited to be truly understood. It's just one of the many ways that this job makes me feel isolated.

Now I really understand multitasking … and it has fried my brain! The stuff you do at an office job is not multitasking. Rubber bands deteriorate over time as they are stretched, pulled, and wrapped around things again and again. The stay-at-home parent's brain should be studied in laboratories! If I sound a bit nutty, if the stress seems to be coming through the pages (or computer screen), that's because I'm here on the battlefield. PTPD … Post Traumatic Parenting Disorder, should be in the medical books.

Much like incessantly changing weather can wreak havoc on some peoples' moods and energy levels, I find the constant seesaw between anger and guilt utterly debilitating. When my children drive me to the edge, I shout at them and then feel so guilty. At first, I didn't know why I was so tired all the time. I was crankier after a day at home with the kids than when I worked in an office, and my wife was perplexed. This was supposed to be invigorating and fun, right?

At work I was only responsible for myself. But at home with three kids, I found that I was constantly assessing all sorts of hazards (Where are the knives and cleaning supplies? Are they high enough?) and monitoring slowly escalating conflict over toys, which would certainly lead to war if I didn't intercede. I cannot emphasize enough how this frazzled my brain. Having to be completely present and focused on multiple things simultaneously was incapacitating.

It has occurred to me that maybe I'm just too sensitive, and that I suck at multitasking. Could this be why staying at home with the kids is so hard for me? I feel guilty for getting frustrated so often. I worry that my kids will think that I don't like taking care of them; which is the furthest thing from the truth. As a disclaimer; I'd like to add that I am well aware that I'm just a fledgling, both as a stay-at-homer and as a parent in general.

As the story progresses, some of you might think that I'm a bit of a control freak and make this job more difficult than it should be. These are my experiences and interpretations, viewed through the lens of someone who is still trying to figure it all out. I'm sure there are better ways of navigating this minefield of tantrums, pee, vomit, cracker crumbs, and Lego foot injuries but I'm working with what I have. I'm also doing my best to sift through the frustration and enjoy the snuggles, relationship-building, and memory-forming that this opportunity has given me.

However, if there's one thing I know for sure, it's that unless someone has stayed home and looked after young children full time, they will never truly understand how difficult it is. From the other side of the fence, this job looks completely different. After proofreading the first draft, I was worried that I sounded like a whiner.

Was I being too negative? Will I seem like a guy that doesn't love his kids? No; if you've been in the trenches as a home-parent, I think you'll understand where I'm coming from.

How did it all happen? Previous to my new vocation, I had been in Human Resources for over two decades. I'm forty-seven, which is on the older end of the dad scale; given that I had my first child at forty-one. My wife is ten years younger and makes good money contracting so the decision as to who stays home was mainly financial. I'll get to the why later. However, I was eager to stay home because I'm a writer on the side and was hoping that this daddy day care gig would give me more time to turn it into a career.

The book I released on Amazon almost two years ago really took off and became a best seller. I wanted to adapt the book into a screenplay. My initial thoughts were that I couldn't really get fired from a home-dad job and the stress wouldn't be as great because I didn't have to deal with commuting, clients, colleagues, and a boss. I figured that I could pump out a screenplay in record time and also build a more solid relationship with my kids. How could I have been so presumptuous? This was the granddaddy of all miscalculations!

When I was working in an office, I'd get up at 3:30am to write as that was my highest creative time. I know that sounds a bit crazy but anyone with kids will tell you that it's utterly impossible to focus on ANYTHING when they are awake, so cutting into my sleep was the only option. After shaking out the cobwebs and downing some coffee, I was good to go for two full hours. However, the sleep deprivation made me a wee bit cranky (or so I'm told) and the idea of being a home-daddy meant (theoretically) that I wouldn't have to get up so early and that I'd have even more time to write. NOPE ... NOPE ... NOPE

I tried and tried to make time for screenplay study and writing but my new job was like an avalanche. I couldn't keep my head above the snowdrifts and became increasingly frustrated. My creative side wasn't being fed and I became despondent. Sure, I'm super-lucky to be home with the kids, but there is more to me than just officiating toy-battles and wiping bums. I was at the same impasse as when I was working in HR; little time and energy for writing ... except that being home was even harder!

I'm writing this book out of sheer necessity. It's therapy. The only way I can get to my screenplay is by typing out my frustrations and coming to terms with the fact that full time home-parenting isn't what I thought it would be.

The idea is that once this catharsis is complete, I'll be able to settle into a rhythm and get the most out of my precious time with the kids and continue to do what keeps me sane … writing.

Hey; call me weak, call me a whiner … oh well. This job is truly exhausting, but I love my kids to the end of the universe and back and wouldn't have it any other way. However, surely there must be a happy medium, the best of both worlds is achievable; isn't it? By sharing what I've learned (so far) on this journey, I hope to find out.

I'll tell you one thing right off the bat; after one year of doing this, I've come to learn that home-parents are made to feel invisible. This is so ironic because without the next generation, there is no future! To people who work regular jobs, I'm a guy that doesn't know how lucky he is. However, to those who look after children full time, I'm speaking the truth.

Introduction

Who is this book for? Just about anyone, really. Never planning on having kids? No problem; this story will give you an idea of what your own parents likely went through! It might also prompt you to be more vigilant with contraceptives. But of course, this book will be of interest to parents of current little ones, teenagers, and adults. Once you have kids, regardless of age, they will always require degrees of parenting. At the very least, they will need money, advice, and free babysitting.

I'm not the stay-at-home dad that rebuilds car engines or makes things in the wood shop. This story is about the daily stuff that any home-parent would go through. It's not a male-oriented take on childcare but rather a gender-neutral account of the outer and inner struggles that occur in the very isolated world of a SAHP (stay-at-home parent). FYI- I'll be using that acronym going forward.

My experiences may or may not parallel yours, and the variables which determine how your kids will behave are infinite. You name it; genetics, culture, environmental factors, etc. all play a part in how your progeny turn out. Some parents get an Antichrist. Some kids are just more difficult than others. If you get an Antichrist, just watch The Omen (the original, not the remake) and you'll feel better.

That being said, my book is definitely not a parenting manual. I am not a qualified kid expert. I'm just a guy who is lucky to be able to spend a lot of time with his children; learning from this amazingly valuable experience while simultaneously being mentally and emotionally pummelled each and every day. My brain has been stretched in every direction and ruthlessly stomped on by these adorable little creatures. However, I'm of the opinion that our kids owe us nothing. I've come to learn that they have given us the gift of being able to teach and nurture another being.

I'm a big believer that levity is a necessary ingredient for sanity, so you'll find humour aplenty in this book. How else could I cope? Well; coffee, alcohol, and exercise are important too, but I find a bit of maniacal laughter the perfect antidote to all of the stressful and kooky situations in my kid-world. Randomly bellowing lines from cartoon movies as I prepare fruit platters is helpful too.

"Sponge Bob has blood." What? One time I had a blocked ear from a kid swimming pool party and Zoe, my 4-year old, kept saying this from the back seat of the car and I just couldn't understand her. I craned my head around and finally deciphered the random child-speak. Alrighty then; Bob the sponge does have blood. Anyway; that's just an example of the usual laughs which also include getting peed and puked on. You too? No kidding!

What will be covered in this memoir of toys, cartoons, and grocery store tantrums? I'll be taking you into the bizarre and often treacherous world of a SAHP... remember; stay-at-home parent. You'll join me in my daily routine; which is very much like working a split shift, except that there's another job in the middle of the high stress shifts on either end. As an aside; I'd estimate that four to six hours of a SAHP's day equals eight hours of an average office job. So, the life of a home-parent is actually comprised of jobs within jobs.

I'll talk about the morning rush, school and day care centre drops, shopping and cleaning, afternoon pick-ups, and of course the Witching Hour. What's that, you ask? It's after school, when they all tumble through the door like modern day Visigoths sacking Rome. They drop their jackets and lunchboxes wherever and demand food. The Witching hour is coffee time! Will I hit the wall and have a meltdown of my own? You'll see…

I'm prone to a good deal of self-analysis, so aside from giving you a day-in-the-life perspective, I'll also share how this job has affected my psyche. Coming from the world of Human Resources, I was very comfortable analysing other people, but now I look into the mirror and point that psychometric beam at the barely recognizable wolfman-looking guy staring back at me. I do try to be objective, but who knows? My better half just says I sound like a housewife that loses her sh*t about every little thing. If you haven't had kids … FYI; they can drive the most even-keeled person to the edge of the abyss.

The analysis chapters will include parental guilt (Do the dishes or play with the children?), my marriage (cough, cough), isolation (a very real issue), and my sense of identity as a SAHP. I also discuss Parent Twitter as well as include some pointers for brand new parents or those waiting for their first velociraptor to hatch. The old saying about kids not coming with a user manual is of course true and my book might be no more useful than Ikea furniture assembly instructions, but I'm sure you'll at least get a kick out of it.

As previously mentioned, I'm writing this as an outlet; a way to cope with domestic stresses I hadn't anticipated. If you're a parent, then I'm sure you will appreciate my effort at catharsis. Just being able to complain to the other kid wranglers during school pickup has been a great release. However, I think that putting this all into words and sending it through the interwebs will give me a sense of peace so that I can truly enjoy this chapter of my parenting journey.

Welcome to my house; and since you're here, would you mind if I popped out for a coffee? I promise I'll be back in a few minutes … or four hours. What's the difference, right? That's what my wife and I do to her sister when she visits! After about half an hour, she'll start texting us asking where we are, and we just sit there in the car giggling. I wish there were more sisters to rotate through.

The Nanny-Go-Round

As I mentioned in the preface, my wife (Louise) and I both used to work full time. When we got together in late 2011, Louise already had her daughter, Beth, who was five at the time. Up until that point, I didn't know the joys of parenthood. When we had Emily in late 2013, Louise went on maternity leave and I continued to work.

I was laid off the following year and since the opportunity was there, we decided that I should give daddy day care a whirl. As a harbinger of things to come, Emily came down with a sudden fever on my very first day. I sent photos of the fever-spots to Louise. The ambulance was there within an hour. Talk about stress! However, my first home-dad stint wasn't very long as Louise soon fell pregnant with our daughter, Zoe. She went back on maternity leave and I had to go back to work.

Following Louise's maternity leave, we decided to get a nanny. Our first one was good. She was a single mom in her late thirties. She made birthday cakes on the side, and although we thought she might be a secret boozer (now I understand), there were no issues. We never had any reason to believe that she drank while looking after our children, but we noticed a consistent supply of bourbon and an impressive collection of horror movie DVD's. We suspected that was her method of unwinding after a day of watching very young, very busy children.

The next year, we moved farther out into the suburbs and had to find someone else. We were lucky enough to hire an older lady who really clicked with the kids. She was from my wife's native country (South Africa) so the shared values and background were an added bonus. Unfortunately, several months later our nanny's husband was transferred, and we were back in the market for a caregiver.

We considered trainees from the city nanny college as well as foreign au pairs. However, the local nanny service lined up some interviews, so we shelved the other options.

After three meetings, we settled on the one that our kids seemed to have the best rapport with. This particular nanny lived in the area, so she would come to our house each morning.

After a few months, Beth, our eldest, started telling stories of boyfriend visits. We were lucky to have an older kid that could be our eyes and ears. After some inquiries, we confirmed that this nanny was stopping by her ex's jobsite with our children. We put an end to the unauthorized trips but sure enough it happened again, so we terminated her contract. And thank goodness our kids were not harmed.

The thing with nannies is that you always have to be scanning for signs of poor performance. Yes; we thought of nanny cams but were exhausted all the time and kept forgetting to do some research. Also; we were concerned about them finding the cameras. If this happened, would the mutual trust, and thus their performance, begin to unravel? Louise and I decided to put the surveillance idea on hold. We had to find a new nanny ASAP.

We revisited the au pair and nanny college options and began by Skyping a girl who lived up north. She was seeking to enrol in the trainee programme and needed on-the-job experience as well as a place to live. We also Skyped two German girls who were moving here in about a month. However, there was concern around the language barrier and the fact that they would have to learn to drive on the other side of the road. These were considerable risks and of course they didn't sit well with us. The girl from up north was available sooner and was born here, so we selected her and converted a storage room into a bedroom.

Some of you might be wondering why we even considered a trainee nanny over someone more experienced. There are pros and cons to both, though. We thought a trainee would be excited about a new vocation and easier to teach our way. We've found that older nannies are more prone to ignoring parents' directives and doing things their way. This was the case with the older lady that moved out of the area and the cake-making (possible) secret boozer nanny that we had in the beginning. Both were much more experienced but often conveniently disregarded certain instructions, which irked us.

This live-in, trainee nanny worked out well in the beginning. She attended the nanny college one day a week and completed coursework online at night. We had the kids in day care on her school day. She integrated well with the family and took our spare car to explore the area on weekends. Unfortunately, she seemed to become disengaged about four months in. We noticed that she was intermittently missing diaper changes and Beth said that she spent a lot of time on her phone texting or talking to an estranged boyfriend.

One weekend I noticed something in the grass, just over the fence. It was a piece of missing Tupperware that had somehow been melted. We asked the kids, but they didn't know how it happened. Later, when the nanny came into the kitchen for a sandwich, we asked her. She said that she used it to heat something up in the oven, but it started to melt so she threw it over the fence. She then became embarrassed and hurried away without further explanation. Huh? I guess she wasn't paying attention during cooking class at nanny college.

We sat her down for a meeting and she admitted to being lax with diapers and spending too much time on the phone, etc. We asked her about the Tupperware again and apparently, she didn't know that it shouldn't go in the oven. Whoa! She apologized, and we let it all slide as she would be graduating the next month and moving overseas. Despite the issues, we parted ways amicably and she's still in touch with my wife via Facebook.

What to do now? Hire an au pair whose primary language is not English and drives on the other side of the road? Another nanny college trainee? Those were concerning options. Eureka! Our previous nanny (the older one) had moved back into the area and was available immediately. Easy-peasy; we were back in business. However, after a few months, we noticed some decay on Zoe's front teeth. We asked Beth how much sugar the nanny was giving her. This was going to be a huge problem.

We found out that candy was an easy way for the nanny to placate Zoe, who (at that time) was three, and whined about everything. So, we asked her to cut back on the sugar. However, she had also become a family friend, and dealing with an older adult is different than giving an eighteen-year-old a firm directive. She agreed, but the sweet treats continued. And if it wasn't candy, it was sugar-laden junk food. What to do? We were in a state of emergency.

I suggested to Louise that since she made more money and I was tired of Human Resources anyway, that we tell the nanny I couldn't stand my job and wanted to stay at home with the kids. After all, I'd done this before, albeit for a short period of time and with one less child. After some intensive discussion which included logistics and number-crunching, we agreed to move forward with this plan. We gave our nanny a month's notice and I did the same at work. I told my boss about the sugar-nanny and that she had to go. I also said we were tired of revolving babysitters and that this was a great opportunity for me to bond with my kids. New Zealand is really big on putting family first, so my boss was understanding.

This is a small region of a small country (one degree of separation; literally) and our little fibs were necessary to keep the peace and maintain alliances. The older nanny is still a family friend. The excessive sugar was really just misdirected grandmotherly affection. Regarding work, I might very well need my old boss for a reference down the line. Perhaps some of you would have been more direct if you were in that situation, but given the cultural dynamics here, it was the wisest move for us.

Anyway, it was time to get off the nanny-go-round. I was now super-dad! Here's the bottom line. No matter who you are or where you're from (barring extenuating circumstances) nobody is going to take better care of your kids than you. I'm well aware that not every parent has the opportunity to do this, but we ran with the best option we had, given our situation. I was excited … I thought this would be easy!

Before we get into the nitty-gritty, I'd like to share that during my first two days of daddy day care I was puked on outside the movie theatre and peed on at gymnastics practice. Ominous signs indeed.

Morning Shift

For me, a relatively insanity-free morning starts the night before. You can't really control what happens once they're awake, but you can at least run the dishwasher and find miniature clothing while they're asleep. After a brain-scarring day of kid wrangling, I know it's hard to muster the energy to do anything. However, it just snowballs endlessly if you don't get ahead of the curve while the opportunity is available. If there were dirty dishes in the kitchen and no clean clothes for the morning, I wouldn't be able to sleep anyway.

I cannot tell you how many times we've started the day with pee-soaked beds and/or fighting over toys. Not two different toys, mind you, but the EXACT same toy! How is this possible? Welcome to the Twilight Zone, Barbie in Some Dreamhouse style. I looked at the Barbies in question ... they were identical! But Emily (five years old) wanted the one that Zoe (remember; four years old) had and insisted it was the better Barbie. WTF! We were then transported to Bedlam.

Imagine all of that going on without clean bowls to serve the oatmeal in or a clean pair of LOL Doll tights, which were the only tights Emily was going to wear that day. Anything that can be done the night before, try to do it. Except dropping the kids off at school ... that's illegal. Having them sleep in their car seats, all dressed and ready, might work though.

Some folks say that they thrive on stress and deadlines; that it brings out the best in them. Not me. I explode into bits of confetti under stress; especially unnecessary stress ... stress that could have been avoided. Ok, maybe I'm not that edgy but let's just say that I build 'moats' around my reactions to stress. These moats take the form of preparation. Anyway; save yourself an aneurism and try to be ready. On the other hand, that might not be your personality type. You might enjoy the free-flow method. If that works for you, awesome ... but I'd be in a straitjacket.

As an aside; stress attacks are frightening for me because unlike at an office job, a SAHP can't pretend to work when feeling overwhelmed. You can't decide to take long bathroom breaks, chat with colleagues while sending unnecessary e-mails, or duck out for three coffees the last half of the day. With kids; you're on ... no excuses, no escape! This is why I'm so careful about building all sorts of stress-protection into my routine. It doesn't always work but I have to try.

Ok, here we go! First up is entering the (already clean) kitchen. Am I harping on too much about preparation? I have prune juice (constipation zaps my energy) coffee, and then a smoothie about twenty minutes later. Too much solid food before late afternoon makes me sleepy. Then I deliver coffee to Louise in bed ... I'm the morning person of the couple. Next is unloading the dishwasher. From there, I begin making lunches and breakfast. I liken this to a dance and try to do it as sequentially as possible, so it all gets locked into my brain and then I can go on autopilot ... until the kids wake up.

If there's one thing I miss about working in an office, it's autopilot. After a while, certain things can be done with very little mental energy and you get something of a 'working break', if that makes sense? Clearing e-mails, banter with colleagues, filing paperwork, etc. With these activities, you can often go to a warm and snuggly place in your mind for a 'virtual nap'. Your workmates manage themselves and you're free to manage you. That's not the case with children. As a parent, you are a manager of others and must be present 100% of the time. Let's get back to the morning shift.

When the first kid wakes up, I quickly activate the 'cartoon sequence'. If a sleepy child walks past a blank TV, they will find you in the kitchen and ask to help with breakfast. That's a weekend activity; I have no time for an assistant during the school week. If the cartoon sequence isn't activated, you've lost 20-30 minutes which could require aspirin or an escape ticket to Panama. I might have to run away and start again with a vasectomy! No, I could never do that to my little buddies … but it has crossed my mind. Also, to be clear, I would get the vasectomy done before going to Panama … highly questionable healthcare.

Sometimes I activate the cartoon sequence before they are awake. I mute the sound but have something on Netflix ready to go. Then, when the first one makes their presence known, I turn up the volume and it acts as a tractor beam to place them in front of the

TV while I'm engaged in kitchen warfare. If we had a difficult time getting them to sleep the night before, and they were up later than usual, I might have to blast the volume to wake them up. I have multiple options all locked and loaded depending on the circumstances.

The goal is to have a peaceful morning with compliant children who are willing to eat their breakfasts, get dressed, and brush their teeth without making any sort of a fuss. Yes; I want a miracle. Needless to say, things don't always go according to plan, hence the alternative options which are designed to get us back on track after a derailment. The endgame is a timely drop-off sequence, so I can make the most of my time alone. More on that later.

My kitchen is my workspace, the office, if you will. While Beth is glued to her laptop watching some teen show, and Emily and Zoe are in Netflix Kids land, I'm working on finishing up with breakfast and lunches. While the oats are bubbling, I'm putting sandwiches together and keeping an ear out for flare-ups over whose turn it is to pick the next cartoon. I also transfer the day's miniature clothing (selected the night before) from the laundry room to the coffee table near the TV. We have an entire room dedicated to the mountains of clean clothes needed to keep these little dribblers and spillers in business.

Putting their clothes in front of them before breakfast plants the seed that the next step after eating is dressing. I try to do everything in sequence so as to condition them on a subconscious level. Every little bit of an edge will help me avoid pandemonium. There will be days of chaos that can't be avoided because after all, we're dealing with children. Nonetheless, everything I do has a purpose. I know myself. I know that when things get crazy, I lose focus and the kids smell it like blood in the water.

The period after breakfast is what I call tantrum reef … the danger zone for resistance over completing some part of the morning routine. If the tantrum shark bites, I'm going to be mentally limping for the rest of the day. For me, kid meltdowns are the biggest energy drain because I also have one. Sometimes it's an internal (repressed) adult meltdown, and other times it's an externalized tantrum like the kids have. Either way, the result is that I've got a stress hangover that might not go away until bedtime. At all costs, do what you can to minimize the potential for these stress bombs.

For example; Zoe recently spilled her oatmeal all over the rug, which was brutal to clean up. I lost it and shouted, then she lost it and cried. This was a physically and emotionally challenging start to the day. In those situations, you can just let go and decide to take your time and be late for school or you can freak out and try to make it before the bell. I've gone both ways. It's never easy; we can only do our best. I'm sure most of you have been there too.

While they finish eating, I'm putting school bags in the trunk and then setting up toothbrushes, floss, and cups for swishing and spitting. Some of you may disagree, but I don't do the teeth-brush sequence in the bathroom. Beth does her own teeth, of course, but Emily and Zoe will be much more agreeable if this is done in the living room while they are watching TV. Yes, the path of least resistance might not pay long-term dividends, but I don't have time to mess around in the morning.

However, before we can get to the teeth, I have to move them through breakfast quickly and without arguments. By quickly, I mean 'kid quickly'. As I'm sure you know, children don't really have a sense of time or urgency. If they weren't prodded a bit, we'd never get out of the house. Most days, they eat at a reasonable pace but on others, instead of eating, they 'dine'. It's like Sunday brunch at The Great Gatsby's house or Rockefeller estate. They move along like trust fund brats without a care in the world; and I'm the butler. Ok; breakfast is over … let's get those teeth brushed.

I bring a face towel as well as the aforementioned spit and swish cups, floss, and loaded toothbrushes. Then I plop down in front of them while the cartoons are going. Emily is cute; she raises her hand whenever I'm brushing too hard. She has sensitive teeth. Zoe can be a little sh*t and often requires a time-out before she'll submit to a teeth cleaning. Then I dress them as quickly as possible, always keeping an eye on the clock.

Oh; I keep alternate outfits at the ready, as kids are prone to refusal of certain clothing items for NO reason whatsoever! Well, at least no logical reason.

"The tag makes you itchy? Ok; I'll tear it off."

"Nope, I just don't like them."

"But you wore those pants three days ago."

"I don't like them anymore."

"But that's the only clean pair in the house without holes."

"No; I won't wear them."

And so the conversation goes. Anyway; be prepared. Better yet, give them a choice to create the illusion of control. Not them, you.

Morning Shift

Parents aren't really in control, are we? Well; we should be, but all moms and dads know that the line moves, and things get murky when stress is afoot.

*Update: What you've just read about tooth brushing in the living room and me dressing them was all happening while I was writing the first draft. Since then, the little ones have been brushing in the bathroom and dressing themselves, for the most part. Two to three days out of five, there is still hemming and hawing over these daily tasks but at least we've made progress! Excruciatingly slow, perhaps, but we are moving in the right direction. Kid-time is funny; on one level it seems to move in slow motion, and on another it's like a blur. You wonder if they're ever going to be proficient with certain tasks and then all of a sudden, they make a big leap development-wise and you can't remember how it happened.

Ok; we're almost finished. Ponytails are the last step before getting into the car. I don't do hair though; that's Beth's job. I tell Louise that I haven't attended the training class. I did suggest the vacuum cleaner thing on YouTube, but Louise has a germ issue. Have a look; you just put the hairband over the vacuum tube, turn it on and then pop the hairband off when the hair gets sucked in … eureka!

Update: I still haven't mastered hair, but it's on my to-do list. Quite often, there's fighting over accidental hair pulling or missing hairbands, so it's in my best interest to figure this out instead of leaving it to Beth. I have a hair block; not sure why.

In the meantime, I'm putting on my dad-jeans, polo shirt, and baseball cap. This is my uniform. I never leave the house without a collared shirt. This garment keeps me from being mistaken as one of the assorted weirdos that make their way about town while the nine-to-five people, the people with the easy jobs, are at work. There are some seriously bizarre people out there. It's like an alternate universe full of old folks, stay-at-home moms, and the Dawn of the Dead kooks. I'm sorry, but if you've seen them, you'll understand.

Ready to go? Wait! Poos? Wees? Three quarters of the time, regardless of how often you reminded them earlier, somebody will have a bodily function requirement the MOMENT you try to leave. See if you can build that into your schedule. I know it's not always possible but give it some thought. Leaving early is a myth but leaving on time is an achievement worth striving for.

Ok; we load into the car and it's off to school first. The day care drop-off window is

Morning Shift

more flexible but you've gotta be at school on time or it's late slip city. As soon as the car stops, Beth is off like a shot as twelve-year-olds don't get walked to school by their parents! I give Emily her backpack, then strap Zoe into the pram, as it's called here, and away we go.

Sometimes Zoe insists on walking and then halfway there, insists on not walking and has a meltdown in front of all the parents and kids whizzing by on scooters and bikes. Those damn scooters! Anyway; even if Zoe wants to use her two little feet, I carry the pram under my arm in the event of a walking strike. After we deliver Emily to her classroom, it's off to the day care centre. Heading back to the car is easier because all of the kids (and their damn scooters) are off the sidewalk.

Update: Zoe now rides her little glide-bike on the school run. No more pram! It was a Christmas gift and she LOVES it! It doesn't have any pedals; I'm sure you've seen them. She quickly pushes and then glides … so cute. She uses her sneakers as brakes; Flintstones-style. Not so great for sneaker longevity, but you can't win em' all. This is a great source of exercise too, as all of that cumulative energy-burning helps keep the dreaded Witching Hour less chaotic … hopefully.

Arriving at the day care centre is a hoot. As we open the door, we're met by an assortment of little chocolate-smeared kids with boogies pulsating from their noses and clothes on backwards. It's like a junior zombie movie. We sign Zoe in and unpack the schoolbag. Usually, she needs a hand-off to her favourite day care lady as she's still clingy. You have to transition them into the day care universe. We stop at the various activity tables and see which one will flip that switch in her brain. Once it happens, I'm pretty much invisible to her.

At first, I felt guilty for leaving Zoe there as part of the reason I decided to stay home with my daughters was to spend more time with them. Beth and Emily had to go to school but not Zoe. I was home now and thought that I should be spending all of that time with her. However, I realized that kids need to be around other kids and go through the socialization process. I know that some parents might disagree on this point, but it seems right to me. I also knew that I needed personal time to get stuff done quickly before the three o'clock Witching Hour when they're all home. Zoe has one half day and one full day off from day care during the week, so plenty of time for us to hang out. Ok; morning routine and drop-offs complete!

Free Time (Not!)

How I spend my so-called free time really depends on the day of the week. I keep it structured to maximize efficiency. Don't get me wrong, there's always that impulse to dilly-dally. After all, SAHP's deserve chill time to recover from the extremely intense morning shift. Because there aren't people all around me doing the same thing (like in an office, for instance) it can be extra challenging to self-motivate and accomplish things. In fact, depression lurks … and it's terrifying. I'm sure you understand.

I've noticed that the silence of a house full of kid paraphernalia (toys, miniature clothes, etc.) without the kids is quite eerie at times. It creates a dangerous vacuum (pun sort of intended) that can derail your to-do list. A couple of times in the beginning, I succumbed to eating myself into a coma and napping or binge-watching Netflix shows. However, the Witching Hour punishment I received later in the day set me straight. Relaxing now, knowing that you're going to get demolished later wasn't for me.

If you don't get certain key things done before the kids get home, they likely won't get done and then you're screwed. Children can always tell when you are behind the eight ball and that's when all sorts of extra neediness arises. No thanks; too brain-scarring for me. I shudder just thinking about that kind of stress. I'll take you through the Monday-Friday mid-shift (i.e. kids not home) before getting into the dreaded Witching Hour. Boo! Yes … it's spooky.

Barring extenuating circumstances, Mondays are my laundry catch-up day. After multiple loads on Monday, one per day the rest of the week is generally all that's required. It's an endless cycle, as I'm sure you know. Everything a SAHP does is an endless cycle. However, your sanity depends on establishing some sort of a routine to keep the madness at bay. Paradoxically, the routine also creates some of the madness. The kids, of course, handle the rest. If you're a current SAHP, you'll understand. If you are a former home-parent, you might not remember.

Monday is also vacuuming day, which is no small job with three kids. The crumbs seem to breed. I'm not talking about big crumbs being smashed into smaller crumbs, but actual breeding. Where do they come from!? Also; no matter how many times you tell them to eat their snacks at the dining room table, they inevitably sneak over to the TV … an inch away from the screen. Crumbs galore. Our vacuum needs to be emptied often. This particular job is compounded by the necessity for picking up all the toys before starting the old Hoover.

As I mentioned in the preface, part of the reason for me staying at home was to have more time for writing. While doing the household chores, I market my other book via social media. This can be done with a phone as I move from one task to another. The book revenue contributes to our income, so I do take this seriously and try to be consistent. It also helps me feel somewhat connected to the outside world.

Unfortunately, I've had trouble finding quality time to do actual writing. After the morning chaos and brain stomping, I'm not in my best creative space. Also; having laundry, dishes, and toys everywhere staring at me in the broad daylight is a huge distraction. A four o'clock wake-up is still the more productive option, but it's hard to flip that switch once you're out of the groove. The exhaustion I've experienced since starting this job is very unusual. I still struggle with rising early, whereas it was pretty easy while working in an office.

     Mondays can also consist of grocery top-ups and other stuff, but what I've just mentioned can easily take up all of my time. On Tuesdays, Zoe has a short kindergarten session, so my opportunity for completing chores and errands is limited. I do laundry, unload/load the dishwasher, and chop vegetables for dinner, etc. It's critical that I also squeeze in a workout and try to do some writing as the after-effects of these activities energize my psyche for the challenges of kid-time.

     The old adage, know thyself, is so very important here. You know what you need to cultivate an energetic, positive mood, right? Do what makes you happy so that you can be the best mom or dad possible. Remember; you're not just a servant. Our non-parental sides must be nourished. If we're miserable, our kids will pick up on that and it will have a negative effect on them.

     Don't get me wrong; when you're depressed or otherwise in a rut, it can be very difficult to kick-start the engine with mind and body exercise. Sure, it sounds like a good idea to do these things but getting through all of the gunk in our systems can feel like an impossible task. It just makes you want to nap, watch TV, and binge when the kids aren't there. I hope that didn't sound too preachy. Depression is a scary thing and I do my best to avoid going near the precipice.

Yes; I went off on a tangent there. Being alone makes me wax philosophical. Back to the Tuesday routine. I pick Zoe up at twelve thirty and we go back home. She finishes her lunch and watches TV while I continue to do chores and keep her entertained. We also eat pistachios together which is a special ritual for us. She loves the challenge of opening them. Despite the fact that there's always something to do to keep the house running, I try to spend a little quality time with the kids. All SAHP's know that it's a struggle to keep the balance between house, kids, and personal needs.

Wednesday is Zoe's off-day from kindergarten. That's our full day together. It took a while to find the right formula where she's kept active enough and I still have time to accomplish the bare minimum to keep the house in order. Four-year-olds are very busy and can't entertain themselves for long. They always need something. They see that you're running around the house and want attention, so they start making requests. This doubles the time it takes to do things but as long as you expect it, the frustration isn't so bad. First, we do the morning routine as usual. Following the school run, it's back to the house where I have a quick shower before we head off to gymnastics.

Zoe gets to bounce and tumble all of that copious energy out of her system. It's an assisted session for younger kids, so I'm on the floor with her and all of the other parents and their little ones. Dads are rare, but I do sight them occasionally. After gymnastics, we usually head over to the adjacent park and play for a bit. Then we go home to have some pistachios together while watching cartoons. As Zoe finishes her lunch, I do laundry and/or dinner prep.

At about twelve thirty, I let Zoe know that we're going to take a nap. She usually says no, but I bring out the magic tool of negotiation … chocolate. My favourite cafe gives a free chocolate with each coffee and I store them in the fridge. I hide these gems behind stuff like broccoli and bags of salad. I show Zoe the sweetie and say that she can have it after the nap. This works like a charm and off we go for a short rest.

Free Time (Not!)

If I'm lucky, I can get a thirty to forty-five-minute recharge. That's all our timetable will allow for due to the school pickup. This is the only day that I nap as I just can't sleep on the other days. Sure; I have the opportunity to, but I won't do it. As mentioned previously, there's just too much to do and it would stress me to the max to leave everything until the kids get home. However, on Zoe's full day off, it makes sense to have a short nap, and the break does help me a great deal.

Some of you might be thinking that this guy could have a much easier time if he just napped for a bit every day; not just on Wednesdays. Do I create a lot of this stress I've been going on and on about? Maybe you're right. However, I've tried it the other way and I'd just get depressed. Without some sort of creative focus, I'd be miserable. I have to push myself toward goals or I'll fall into a pit of depression. On the flipside, this tight schedule does wear me out, but the alternative is much worse. Such is life. Ok; that's my Wednesday … let's move along.

Thursday is my big-shop day. After the school run, I head straight to the mall for an almond milk flat white (as they are called here) and then burst into the grocery store with purpose. But wait! There are old people everywhere! I love old people, they have such wisdom to impart, but they live in slow motion. Out of my way …. please! This is where I employ the zen of grocery shopping technique. The more pissed off you get, the more spaced out and slow the oldies become, so you gotta chill. Can you do that? I do my best. It doesn't always work.

All of the usual suspects are there. Stay-at-home moms, the aforementioned oldies, and of course the zombie squad. There are just some damn weird people out there between nine in the morning and three in the afternoon. Maybe everyone else thinks I'm in the zombie squad. I hope not. I try to look professional, but I don't think home-dads are one of those accepted things within the nine to three collective unconscious. Oh well, I could be wrong.

So, I bomb through the grocery store utilizing my memorized auto-list (the stuff we always need) and phone notes for the bits and bobs that we might only need fortnightly or monthly. If I had the kids with me, I could never be this efficient. I'll cover it in another chapter but suffice to say, do not bring them grocery shopping if it's at all avoidable. You'll leave the store psychologically and spiritually mangled.

Your soul will be half in and half out of your body.

As soon as I get home, I put the food away lightning fast. I try to create this rush rush urgency, stomping in and out. The house is eerily quiet, yet my internal drill sergeant pushes me to hurry up. If I sit down for a moment, the rest of my day is screwed. If I stop to dilly-dally, I won't write, which will leave me feeling like a failure. I won't exercise, which will stunt the creative flow needed for my writing. Everything is tied together, and I must persevere. Yes; I know it sounds extreme, but it works for me.

Once the groceries are put away, I can then do the aforementioned writing and exercising. There's always laundry to do and a dishwasher to load/unload … it's never-ending. Of course, as I type (right now!) the washing machine and dishwasher finish-bells sound. Can you believe it? I'm not kidding. Off to hang it on the line … quickly. If I leave the clothes, I'll forget about them and have to rewash due to that sour milk smell that we get punished with for having SAHP brain. This is why it's better for me to write from four to six in the morning; but I still struggle to get up. Ok; that's my Thursday mid-shift.

It's Friday! Yes; even though I'm a stay-at-home parent, Fridays are still festive. I thought that all days of the week would blur into the same thing, but they haven't. There's just something in the air on Fridays. I remember this feeling when I worked in an office and am glad it hasn't gone away. It's not as euphoric as a city full of people looking forward to their weekends, but I'll still take it. The main theme for Friday is grocery top-up and errands.

Even with a list and no kids to distract me, there's always stuff I forget on the Thursday big shop. Also, I buy wine on Fridays. Why not Thursday? Because I'll drink it all. Just kidding. The errands often include car maintenance and/or supplies for household repairs, as well as picking up specialty items that the grocery store doesn't have. All of these little stops add up, as I'm sure you know. I've tried to fit everything in on Thursdays and it just doesn't work.

After grocery top-up and errands, I do a load of washing (the omnipresent laundry) and any necessary after-school snack prep and/or dinner prep. Then it's writing, book marketing, and an exercise session. By the way, sometimes on a Friday, I do go off the rails and rebel against this schedule. As previously mentioned, it happened more in the beginning, when I was unaware of the consequences. But, every now and again, I just eat everything in sight and sink into a coma for a few hours. Why

Friday? Because we can all finish the errands on Saturday ... together.

It's pretty monotonous and lonely during the middle of the day, but this is the challenge all SAHP's face. 'The grass is always greener' saying comes to mind. I can certainly remember tough days while I was working in an office and thinking how much better it would be staying home with the kids. It definitely is better, but in ways I didn't anticipate. Do you hear the tick-tock of the clock? It's the Witching Hour! Batten down the hatches ... your brain is gonna be toast!

The Witching Hour

The Witching Hour exists in another dimension. It's like a place in the forest where sunlight doesn't penetrate, and the absence of birds chirping is a sure sign of doom. However, there is also a wisp of excitement because your lonely walk in the woods is about to be livened up. Is this a fairy tale? No, the kids will be home soon, and Bedlam will reign! Seriously; the Witching Hour is scary!

Every SAHP knows this feeling. The middle of your split shift is fraught with danger as the Witching Hour approaches. If you've evaded the booby traps of couch-surfing or a visit to the beach, you might survive the afterschool madness with only a flesh wound.

Don't get me wrong, self-care is important and of course a home-parent should be allowed coffee with a friend or a binge-watching session of their favourite show. All parents approach this job differently; there is no 'right way'. However, for me, a relaxing mid-shift usually spells disaster. Oh; the Witching Hour doesn't start at home … it starts when you collect the children.

    I pick Zoe up (on her long days) at two-thirty and move stealthily through the day care centre sign-out procedure. Then I continue onto lunchbox, water bottle, and backpack retrieval. As soon as I grab the lunchbox, its weight tells me how much has been eaten. Then I open it up to see what foods were popular that day and if the carnage inside warrants a run through the dishwasher. Ninety-five percent of the time, it looks like the inside of a dirty microwave oven. The ladies at the centre know I'm on a tight timeline as Emily and Beth are next on the pick-up list.

    The above is my plan, anyway. If the day care centre kids are all playing outside, I can usually get away with completing these steps undetected. But if Zoe knows I'm there, I might be intercepted and spun round and round with hugs and kid-chatter. I love hearing about her day, but this must take place in the car or we risk being late for the school pick-up. So, if all of the kids are inside, I have to be extra careful as Zoe might see me as I arrive; or even more likely is spy sabotage.

I try to enter the building like a Jedi; using The Force to be invisible to Zoe's friends. If the Jedi Mind Trick fails, the little spies all point at me (smeared with chocolate, dirt, boogies, and/or paint) and shout, "it's Zoe's daddy!" Then the game is up, and my speedy extraction is in jeopardy. It's really cute though; parent arrival triggering chaos. I suspect this happens on all of the pick-ups, but only the ladies of the centre know such things.

Yes, being home with the kids certainly inspires the imagination. If Zoe is in a good mood and has had her fill of play and kid interaction, we can zoom out of there and proceed to the big-girl school. However, if she's cranky, in the middle of some sort of activity, or just plain old obstinate that day, I'm done for. There are other pitfalls as well. Her shoes and socks could be missing, or she might have spotted me upon arrival and found a hiding place to prank me. Why not just pick her up earlier, you ask? Slack time with a kid is just as perilous as trying to stick to a tight schedule.

If I'm lucky, Zoe will just get into her car seat. I'm usually not that lucky. It's often a long, drawn-out process where she must get to her seat in the most illogical, time consuming manner possible. Why? Because it's fun. Because life is a jungle gym. As her friends' wave goodbye through the window, Zoe knows she's on stage. Waving, jumping, dancing, etc. Once again, why don't I build that into my schedule? Umm; because if we get to the school too early; I'll have to talk to people. But yes, I feel terribly isolated. It's all such a paradox…

Once Zoe's car seat is buckled, we're off to the elementary school. On the way, I listen to her adorable debrief. A four-year-old explaining how their day went often requires the skill of a cryptographer. They ramble away as you try and look for coherent elements to make sense of the semi-gibberish. It's both fascinating and frustrating at this age as their communication skills improve daily. They slowly morph into a new person right before your eyes.

As we get to the street the school is on, I try to park as closely as possible; and of course, the other parents do the same. Some wait in their vehicles and others walk up to the school to collect their mini-me's. This is Emily's first year, so I like to be right outside her classroom when the bell rings. Zoe glides along on her little bike as I follow behind, shouting at her to stop and check the driveways for cars pulling in or backing out.

As we approach, the parents are all there, gathered into little groups and chatting away. I always arrive with no more than a minute to spare. If I'm earlier than that, I stop under a nearby tree and wait until one minute before the bell. Why? Because I'd have to talk to people. And yes; as previously mentioned, I miss adult interaction. I know it doesn't make sense, but if you're a SAHP, you'll likely understand. I guess being alone most of the time makes it hard to break the ice, whereas at a regular job, you're forced into consistent conversation.

The bell rings and out comes Emily to tackle me and speed-talk about her day. It's wonderful to have your kid miss you and give hugs with all of their might. Then Beth appears, as this is our pre-arranged meeting point. She keeps her distance because I'm an 'embarrassing parent'. Or, I'm just a parent and the embarrassing part is a given. She nags to go home immediately but no way; this is my chance to wear the little kids out.

There is a play area right outside of Emily's classroom (There are several classrooms per building at this school.) and most of the kids stay behind and burn off their abundant energy. They say that children need to decompress after a full day of learning, so this saves us a trip to the park. Although it isn't Zoe's school, she's quite popular with Emily's classmates. Neither of my little ones can get across the monkey bars unassisted, so I risk getting kicked in the face while holding their legs. Good times!

Beth either plays with the other kids or tells me about her day in teen-speak, which is a different language than four-year-old speak. Sure, the sentences are more coherent, but cryptography expertise is still required. A teen's universe is all about them and the drama-filled stories you hear must be taken with a grain of salt. Ok; pretty similar to an adult, except the narcissism is more obvious. When the stories get too long, I ask her to tell me what happened, backwards. This way, I get the important stuff first and can half-listen to the rest of it.

Once they all start to nag for food, it's off to the car we go. I purposely do not bring food or water to the pick-up location as that is my way of getting them to agree to head back. I've got vegetables to chop and laundry to dry! I usually announce that the park is closing, and we must hurry, or we'll get locked in with the bears. The other parents hear this and either chuckle or repeat it to their kids and we all have a laugh. Beth rolls her eyes as she knows it's not true, but Emily and Zoe kind of look for the bears.

On our way back to the car, those damn scooters whiz past on all sides. It drives me nuts as kids of varying ages barely miss us while I try to ensure that nobody gets hit. Whether it's after school, in the grocery store, or anywhere else in public, I'm always concerned about my kids getting hurt. As I'm sure most of you know, incessantly worrying about your kids' safety is exhausting.

Once we're back at the car, I give them the extra water and snacks. But once again, I never bring these items to the school or they'll want to play too long. Carrot on a stick, folks. Getting them into their car seats can be a mission, though. They start fighting and/or playing with the dashboard switches as I put the backpacks and Zoe's bike into the trunk. It's usually pandemonium as accusations of spitting and bogey-wiping abound.

Woohoo! We're in the car! After all of that, can't dad have a few minutes to get his bearings and check his phone? Nope; as soon as I buckle myself in and pick up the phone, they start nagging and/or fighting. Hair pulling, water squirting, or cries to use the bathroom keep me from getting a single moment to recharge. It's enough to make you want to voluntarily check into a psychiatric hospital. So, off we go … on our way home and into the belly of the beast.

As the kids spill into the house and plop down on the couch, I quickly have Beth activate the 'cartoon sequence'. This provides enough distraction so I can get the backpacks out of the car and empty those imploded lunchboxes. If this is forgotten, the next morning will be a horror show. Washing lunchboxes by hand is a major hassle. Were they microwaved with banana and yogurt inside? Was the juice of an orange squeezed all over and then mixed with the flavour powder from a packet of sour cream rice crackers and spread evenly with one of their dirty little fingers? Do they do this on purpose? I know, I've complained about it already.

Depending on how much time I've had to prepare for the madness, there might be fruit in the fridge, all cut up and ready to serve. More often than not, though, I frantically tear open a package of their favourite sour cream and chive rice crackers and chuck it over the side of the boat as the feeding frenzy begins. Ok; this isn't Shark Week, but it's pretty close. By the way, I have to divvy out the crackers very precisely or there's trouble. They count everything!

When multiple children are given any type of food, the first thing they'll do is eyeball what the other kids are getting to ensure that everything is 'fair.' The word fair is bandied about quite a bit in our house. I ask them to 'define fair' and they just look at me blankly. But anyway; back to the crackers. Everybody looks at how many they have, and only when they're satisfied that everything is fair, will they dig in.

While we're on this subject; if it's at all possible, serve them snacks/meals in the EXACT same bowls/plates, etc. to support the illusion of fairness. If you make a mistake here; if you give one child an extra something or other, it could spell doom. I'm not kidding. While they're eating or licking their crackers (yes, licking is common) I get to work on the fruit. A little fruit platter will satisfy their afterschool cravings just long enough so that I can make coffee.

After the snack, it really depends on what day it is as far as activities go. On certain days, Beth has dance class, and on others Emily will have gymnastics. The slack time on those activity days is filled with driving all over town. They can be more hectic, but on the flipside, the changing landscape will keep the kiddos distracted enough where they might not fight. Well, might not fight until later. There's always a flareup over something. However, I'll take you through a standard day where it's just us at home after school.

During their afternoon fruit and cracker break is when I usually hit the wall. Coffee is so very important, but for me, proper food intake is critical as well. I've tracked my energy patterns/fluctuations and found that drinking vegetable smoothies in the morning and afternoon will keep me afloat for this incredibly demanding job. Everyone is different, so, as they say, know thy self. I'm sure many of you prefer a full breakfast and lunch. Alternatively, I doubt that fasting would be successful when dealing with the hyperkinetic vibes of children. I just know that solid food sinks me, and no food at all makes me edgy.

Ok; we zigged and zagged a bit, but hey, that's what being at home with the kids is all about. Or, I could be avoiding the hardest part of my day because I've been traumatized by it so many times. Maybe on a subconscious level, even writing about it scares me. Please understand, despite the humour and sarcasm, I love being with my kids. Someday they will be off doing their own thing and I'll be the one chasing them for attention. I know it all goes by fast. A big reason why I wrote this book is to examine my time with these little characters so that I can get the most out of it. Complaining infused with humour is just how I cope. Enough avoidance … back to the Witching Hour.

The Witching Hour

The kids are usually calm for a little bit after their snack so it's extremely important for me to maximize this opportunity. I could be sitting on the couch chilling with them as some sort of cartoon plays in the background, but that's a trap. I've been burned by this before and the consequences are dire. So, instead, I'm either frantically dealing with some phase of the laundry process and/or preparing for dinner.

Like clockwork, Zoe will get bored with the cartoon and begin causing trouble with Emily and Beth. The kids' TV tastes (Netflix tastes, actually) are ever-changing and because she's only four, I think Zoe doesn't always grasp the storylines, so her ability to remain engaged isn't quite at the level of the other kids. That's my theory, anyway. Regardless, she's the first one to start trouble when bored. This is my cue to get them outside, stat!

Depending on the weather, we'll shove off to the park or do a couple of laps around the block on our bikes. As I'm sure you know, kids need a constant infusion of fresh air or they go bonkers. However, it doesn't take long for someone to say they're tired, bored, or need to pee, and then we're back at the house. There might be some colouring in or painting going on while I run the bath for Zoe and Emily. At this point, dinner is almost finished and in the bath they go.

Bath time is full of bubbles and toys. Bubbles, toys, and fighting! They'll be able to shower on their own soon enough but right now, at this age, they must bath together. Unfortunately, it's a combustible situation as playing often quickly turns to kicking, scratching, and tears. If I'm there the whole time, they will behave. But as soon as I leave to check on the dinner, an aquatic melee ensues. Oh well, this is a temporary thing as showering will be much easier. Have them shower separately now; you say? Not yet; we tried that and it's even more chaotic.

Out of the bath they come and into their PJ's. At this point, dinner is on the table and mum is just about to walk in the door. The evening shift will soon begin! After a day punctuated with stressful events, this is usually when I'm at my most frazzled. Back and forth from kitchen to bathroom officiating hair pulling and water fights, taking laundry out of the dryer, and tidying up, etc. I'm toast!

My wife has just had a nice, hour-long train ride home. She's been able to decompress from the workday while scrolling through her phone and/or napping. I, on the other hand, need a freaking brain transplant. However, she still gets miffed when I'm not in the mood to have a little chitchat. I just want to hide away in the bedroom alone (alone, alone, alone) for fifteen minutes to reboot. But how can you relax when you know that more mess is about to be made? Yes; I'm already thinking about the dinner dishes. Wait; I think she's home!

Evening Shift
(or, go the Fu*k to Sleep!)

As soon as my wife walks in the door, I feel this amazing sense of relief. Not because I can tune out for the rest of the evening, but because the kids now have equal points of focus which makes an enormous difference from a mental perspective. When you're doing it all alone for hours on end, the strain can drive even the most patient people over the edge. I am truly in awe of single parents.

So, by the time she arrives, the kids are bathed, and dinner is ready. Only under extenuating circumstances will this not happen. Ok, kids create innumerable extenuating circumstances all throughout the day, but I really do strive to complete these two critical tasks by the time she gets home. I don't think it's cool for the house to be in a state of chaos when she arrives. I do my best. But I'm also a cranky bastard ... or so she says.

Sometimes I'm too stressed out to immediately sit and eat with the family, so I'll call the kids for dinner and disappear to fold laundry. Then I'll show up mid-meal in a better place mentally and have my food. But while eating, I'm thinking about ensuring that the dishes are rinsed (properly) and loaded into the dishwasher and run through before bedtime. Food caked on dishes and silverware overnight turns into cement. This drives me nuts. Yes, I'm a control freak and need to relax. It's hard but I'm getting better.

As any parent knows, a peaceful meal is impossible with young children. As soon as you relax, they want something. Despite anticipating every conceivable need, they'll find a way to disrupt you. Napkin- check. Water- check. Ketchup- check. But rest assured, they'll have a request. Sometimes I just eat standing at the counter because there's no point in sitting down.

The worst is when you make a concerted effort to prepare a nutritious, tasty meal and hear, "yuk". The nerve! But then again, they're usually not hungry because they've been snacking. I've tried telling them to wait until dinner and that being a little hungry will make the meal better, etc. They just nag you to the point of a mental breakdown, so you give them something to keep them quiet and then of course they barely eat their dinner.

We do our best to teach the kids table manners, but they insist on eating mainly with their hands and then rubbing the grease from the meat onto their clean pyjamas! No; bathing them after dinner isn't an option ... it's too exhausting. So, in an effort to keep them from spilling all over themselves or using pyjamas as napkins, I tell them that bugs will smell the food on their clothes and crawl on them at night. It seems to work for a couple of bites, but that's all.

After dinner I'm right back to the kitchen, scraping plates and loading the dishwasher. Preparing for the next day is critical. I know there are some people who leave dishes overnight, but I just can't. I'll walk into that kitchen at six in the morning and start slamming things around; all pissed off because of the mess. As long as I have that dishwasher running and any remaining plates rinsed and stacked for the next load, I'm happy.

As this is going on, Louise and the kids hang out for a while before the dreaded bedtime sequence. This is every parent's hell-zone. Little people never want to go to sleep. We start the process by announcing that bedtime will be in ten minutes. This plants the seed. They grumble a bit and then go back to whatever they were doing. The passive resistance has begun as the kids go strangely quiet.

A child that knows they are close to bedtime will not make a peep. No food requests, no fighting, nothing. They're aware that mom and dad are just looking for any excuse to turn that TV off. Because it's so rare; because having calm, content children is something that we are continually striving for yet rarely experience, Louise and I will enjoy this brief utopia before the final push to get them into bed.

But of course, moments like these aren't meant to last. Despite the fact that six kids could comfortably sit in front of that TV, one will kick or shove the other, trying to be dead-center before the magic talking rectangle. The ruckus yanks us out of that idyllic moment, and we return to business as usual. We announce bedtime. But, of course, it's just not that easy.

You all know the drill. 'I'm thirsty, I'm hungry, I'm not tired, just ten more minutes, just one more episode', etc. You name it, we've heard it. And I'm sure you've heard it all too! So, we shut off the TV and it's to the bedroom we go. A story or two is read before the tuck-in. Tuck-in is critical! Then Louise and I go to bed and wait. Why do we wait? Because the next phase begins. At thirteen, Beth has been around long enough to give up and go to sleep; but not the little ones.

Almost instantaneously, footsteps are heard. Which one is it? Hmm … that cadence means it's Zoe. Cute-face in full force, she arrives at our bed with more requests. She wants snuggles, she's still hungry, she's not tired, she needs her 'noculars' (binoculars) to watch the birds. Louise and I take turns dealing with this. Depending on our energy levels, we either shout or pick her up and carry her back to bed for yet another snuggle.

Minutes later, we hear Zoe and Emily talking. This quickly becomes arguing. It's obvious they are both out of bed. Then we hear screaming, and toys being thrown against walls. Mom and I are tired, and timeouts require extra energy, so we yell from our bedroom. The little insomniacs appear. Other excuses include the blanket not being on correctly and needing help to find a particular stuffed animal to cuddle with. For people who have more sleep requirements than adults, they certainly don't act that way.

By the time Louise and I confirm that they're out cold, we're usually too tired to watch a show together. To have a semblance of a relationship (what's that?) it's critical that you actually spend quality time together … alone. However, the time we get is brief and we're both usually irritated and exhausted by then. So, we lay there in bed and scroll through our phones; until one of us drops it on our face. Have you ever done that?

Well, there you have it, my Monday through Friday routine. It's hard work but it's the most important work. Our childhoods have a staggering influence on the kinds of adults we become. Our outlook on life, temperament, how we communicate, and even our facial expressions can be sourced back to our parents. Every once in a while, I'll make a face or say something and then catch myself and go, 'that's my dad!'

This is why, despite the stress and frustration, we must always remember the impact we have on our kids and be mindful of what we're giving them as examples of how to be adults. Wow, that sounded preachy. I'm actually saying this as a reminder to myself. You don't need the speech; at least not from me. But I need to recite this into the mirror so that my kids get the best of what I can offer … even though I'm often quite grumpy. But then again, the words grumpy and dad go together like peanut butter and jelly, right?

Weekends and School Vacation

Although weekends differ in many ways from vacation time, I thought they should be included in the same chapter because their common thread is the lack of structure that school and/or day care would otherwise provide. For me, structure is critical as I've found that my kids act up if they aren't transitioned into different activities throughout the day. I always have the next thing for them to do in mind and then look for signs that they need a change before chaos erupts. I hadn't anticipated struggling with weekends and holidays but soon learned about the dangers of slack time. Let's start with Saturday and Sunday.

When my SAHP adventure began, I thought that weekends wouldn't matter anymore. I expected each day to blur into the next; much like a retiree. Of course, I was in for a huge surprise. It's one year later, and I still look forward to the weekends just as much, even more actually, than I did working in an office. However, I'm sure everyone's situation is different.

If you have a partner to help with the kids, and that partner actually helps, then I'll bet you love the weekends. But if you're a single parent, Saturday and Sunday are probably extra challenging. Because you are doing it all alone and there is no break provided by day care or school, your weekends might feel like two consecutive Mondays. Then again, you could find it difficult for other reasons; even if you do have help. Maybe, like me, you get quality help on the weekends but are such a control freak that it's hard to see your system get messed up on Saturday and Sunday.

However, despite my kitchen becoming a disaster area on the weekends, I'm thrilled to have the extra help and, more importantly, the company. An adult to talk to, even someone you often squabble with, is a lifesaver when your week is devoid of any meaningful, intellectual conversation. Don't get me wrong, being with my kids all week is a gift unto itself, but my psyche has needs that they are unable to fulfil. Being a parent is a huge part of who I am, but it's not all of my identity. Side-note: I'm really looking forward to philosophical conversations with my kids when they're older.

Weekends start on Friday afternoon, right? The Friday fever hits around three o'clock, and then my parent discipline wanes. Do they really need a bath? Why should I chop vegetables? Look, Dominoes just sent an e-mail … they're running a special! And best of all; wine, craft beer (or both) will be opened very shortly. Yaay! It might be a working weekend, but I'll still take it. Any break in the routine is welcome.

We often do a Friday night movie with the kids. Just so there's a way for me to be more engaged, I'll suggest a youth-oriented 80's flick. Of course, they all make fun of me (Louise is ten years younger) for knowing about these old films, but I tell them that age is just a number as I do a dreadful 80's dance. However, as all parents know, this two-day break is still hard. There will be tantrums, squabbles, and dirty dishes galore; but at least we're all in it together.

Like many two-parent households, we alternate Saturday and Sunday mornings on breakfast and coffee duties. By seven o'clock, someone is awake and standing beside our bed with an adorable, groggy look on their face. What do they want? Food and cartoons. What do we want? A priceless kid-snuggle followed by thirty more minutes of sleep. Actually, how about a sleep-in until noon? And so it begins…

While drinking coffee in bed and scrolling through our phones, we listen to what's happening in the family room as they stream in with requests for more food and screen time. They also tell one-sided stories about who kicked whom or pulled hair, etc. This relative calm won't last long, though. Like the smell of revolution in the streets, there will soon be an eruption and chaos shall reign. The longer we wait, the harder it'll be to get them dressed and out the door. As I'm sure you know, the biggest impediment is parental exhaustion from a long week.

We have risked those 'pyjama days' in the past and were badly burned. I guess it depends on how many kids you have and/or their ages and temperaments, etc. All I know is that with three girls ranging from four to thirteen, all Hell is going to break loose at some point if we don't get them out for some sort of an activity. It might be just thirty minutes at the park, or even a trip to the grocery store, but we

Weekends and School Vacation

HAVE to get them out, or we'll end up fighting with them, and likely with each other.

Once we feed the creatures a second breakfast and grab a quick meal for ourselves, it's time to get them dressed and brush teeth and hair. Because it's the weekend and there's less urgency around leaving at a specific time, the whole process takes at least an hour longer. Although I've mentioned it already; for those of you that haven't had kids (yet) or perhaps have one child, this procedure is usually very lengthy and stressful. The kids know we're not overly concerned with timelines, and they take advantage of it by being extra difficult. Well, they call it having fun.

After choosing our activity and getting the girls loaded into the car, Louise and I always look at each other with this disoriented, worn out look on our faces. We wonder aloud how it took so long to do something so simple. This is our little ritual, and we do it without fail. On the odd chance that we're visiting someone, we'll text them and say we're going to be late. We're always late … to everything.

After our activity of the day, we tumble back into the house and feed the perpetually hungry. Really, all they do is eat and play … what a life! Following a bit of settling in, we plant the seed that naptime is coming. They predictably go quiet and continue munching and watching TV or playing. After announcing naptime again, depending on how receptive they are, we may dangle candy and promise they'll get it when they wake up. Hey, whatever it takes.

Emily often screams that naps are for babies. Well, no pumpkin, not exactly. Naps are for moms and dads. Louise and I covet weekend naps above all else. If we don't get a break, we're screwed. We have no evening and will end up snapping at each other as the kids take advantage of our weariness. You'd think that without an afternoon nap, the children would go to bed earlier. Sorry, as most of you know, that's usually not how it works. In any event, at the very least, we enforce quiet time in their beds with a book while we take turns power napping.

The kids usually wake up groggy, but the pre-nap promise of candy is their very first point of focus. We then get dinner going and pick a family movie. After the movie, it's off to bed and then Sunday comes; which generally follows Saturday's pattern. All-in-all, the weekend is a time for me, the SAHP, to have some help with the kids and work on our relationship, which of course is tested considerably with children. No, it isn't Vegas. It's real life and the payoff is a great relationship with my kids. This (hopefully) includes consistent nursing home visits when I'm old.

Although I look forward to Louise's assistance and camaraderie on weekends, the biggest challenge is losing control over the kitchen and laundry room. Illogical dishwasher load configurations, wet clothes forgotten in the machine that smell like sour milk, and general household items not put back where they belong. All of this drives me mad. Yes, I know, just let it go … and I do my best. By Monday afternoon, logic and order have returned. Sanity, however, is another story.

As previously mentioned, school vacation is similar to weekends in that the kids are home without any sort of formal activity structure. Sure; things like dance and sports camps can help, but this isn't always an option. Also, the dynamic can be quite different depending on whether or not a partner/spouse is available to help during the break. There might be a two-week family vacation over the summer, but in most situations the remainder of the holiday is on the SAHP, as hubby goes back to work.

Every parent knows that when children aren't kept busy, they go bonkers. They nag, fight, and get into all sorts of mischief. Most adults love to kick back on their time off, but kids' little brains need stimulation. The world is new to them and the more they absorb and process, the more they seek out. How do you reconcile a parent's desire to do absolutely nothing and a kid's need to do everything?

I grew up in the 80's and back then, all the kids in the neighbourhood would either play in each other's yards, have a touch football game on the street, or prank golfers at the local course. Near the first hole of the Furnace Brook Golf Club in Quincy, MA there is a big hill which obscures the flag from the tee-off point. We'd wait in the trees near the hole and watch for the balls to sail over the hill and then snatch them before the golfers knew what happened. We'd either keep the balls or put them in the hole and get a kick out of their reactions peeking from nearby bushes. It was a blast!

When it was time to come in, moms or dads would call from their porches, 'Johnny, dinner!' or whatever, and the kids would go home. Simple. Children occupied all day and likely worn out. Not anymore. Well, I'm sure there are still little towns where kids can safely play without supervision. But overall, our fear as parents has risen. Is it because scary news travels so fast due to the internet? In any event, at least for me, those days are over. I keep my kids within ear and eyeshot at all times. As a result of keeping them close, they often drive me nuts. However, there's no way I'd chance the alternative.

As previously mentioned, I found out quickly that kids thrive on structure. They need it or go off the rails. To be fair, most adults (whether they realize it or not) like their routines as well. When school is out, chaos is always banging on your door. Keeping them busy is stressful and requires creativity and flexibility. A framework that can bend when conditions change (and they usually do with kids) is no easy feat.

The only way to keep the chaos mob at bay is a plan. I've been dragged to the gallows far too often to wake up during school holidays and expect the kids to keep themselves harmoniously occupied. The operative word is harmonious. Sure, I could let them play until all Hell breaks loose and then come up with an activity … but by then it's too late. Why? Because their fighting and meltdowns are so exhausting to deal with that I'd be mentally hobbled for the rest of the day.

There's only so long that toys, the TV, and puzzles/games, etc. will keep them happy. I've tried doing arts and crafts with my kids, but they won't let me do anything beyond holding a piece of yarn. They just want me to sit there next to them. I'm not allowed to do anything crafty, but I'm not allowed to leave either. This is SAHP life in a nutshell.

In February of 2019, I completed my first summer break. I learned a great deal, but of course I'm not in a rush for the next school vacation. During the last week of classes, I was complaining (me, complain?) to one of the more experienced parents about how psychologically challenging it was going to be with them home for the entire day without help. As we were waiting for the bell to ring, she mentioned that at least I didn't have to get them up and ready for the school run each morning. Well; there was a ray of light! Maybe this would be easy after all, I naively thought. No; it actually wasn't.

I'm sure everyone is different; but as a SAHP, I ultimately found that having to be places each day at certain times was very important. Without these markers during the school holidays, I was adrift, hypnotized into believing that everything would flow along nicely. Why was I thinking like such an amateur? I had previous full-time daddy day care experience and clocked in plenty of hours on the weekends to know that such an expectation was bonkers. Maybe this was an extreme form of wishful thinking?

It was obvious that our summer vacation needed some structure as all of the slack time was very combustible. They could only last so long with any particular activity before one of them started getting restless and then agitating the others. The kids were in one room and I was in another, trying to get the bed made, use the bathroom alone (yes, alone!), put laundry away or whatever. I was constantly in a state of low-grade panic, scanning for tell-tale sounds, waiting for the first signs of trouble. My PTPD (Post Traumatic Parenting Disorder) was flaring up.

In many ways, school vacation is like a weekend; a very, very long weekend with no partner to share the madness. There isn't another adult to argue with over whose turn it is to go into the living room and break up the tenth squabble over two identical Barbies. Before that nine-week long test of sanity, I had a bit of me-time on most days while the kids were at school/day care. To people who work regular jobs, it would be akin to a commute and/or lunch break. This alone time would be filled with laundry, shopping, cleaning, etc. It wouldn't be chill time, that's for sure. In any event, my little titbits of peace and quiet were gone for over two months.

In addition to the annual nine-week holiday, there are smaller two-week breaks throughout the year. After surviving a couple of these, I've learned a bit about how I react to them, and subsequently, how to operate more efficiently to be the best dad possible for my kids. Aside from sharing my experiences with fellow parents, it's important to re-emphasize that a big reason for writing this book is self-analysis for the purpose of enjoying time at home with my children versus melting down and running back to office work. I don't want to return to paying someone else to raise my bubbies during their formative years.

So; here's what I've learned. Over the past several school vacations, I have observed a pattern develop. The two things that keep my physical and creative engines happily running get derailed when school's out. Because the kids are home all the time, I can't get my workouts in, and there's no opportunity to write. I have tried to get up early for both exercise and writing but it's hit or miss at best. I usually wake up feeling like a train hit me and I've attributed this to the aforementioned lack of personal time during holidays.

By day three or four of a school break, I'm cranky and despondent. It feels very similar to being constipated. I'm completely stuck as all of my usual outlets are inaccessible. Holidays are a golden opportunity to spend even more quality time with my kids yet I'm not at full capacity. The problem, at least for me, is stamina. It's mentally and physically so hard to keep up with them when you don't have the usual intermission provided by school and/or day care. If you're a SAHP, I'm sure you know what I mean.

But hey; it isn't the kids' fault. I should be enjoying this while I can, as I now know that it really does go by fast. I'll soon be yesterday's news. The big wide world will be calling in several years and dad won't be the centre of their universe. Once again … guilt. I feel bad for having to struggle to be at my best for my children. Well; at least I'm trying. At least I'm reflecting on it and working to improve, right?

The next time school holidays come, I'll be prepared and not fall into the lack of structure trap. I'll plan activities ahead of time. I'll also try to go for an early morning run at least once or twice a week to flush my physical energy, and somehow squeeze in a bit of writing time for creative sustenance. Most importantly, I'll do my best to enjoy the extra time off with my little friends and not have brain tissue leak out of my ears from the stress. I saw that brain leak thing on a Bevis and Butthead episode; brilliant!

Summarizing lessons on the kid-end; they need to be fed often and kept busy. Their attention span is short, so a mixture of physical activity, crafts, and games, all interspaced with snacks and full meals is critical. Of course, everyone's situation is different. So, take from this what you will, and/or exclaim 'I already knew all of that!' Ha ha; it's still nice to peer into someone else's house though, right? Good luck on your next vacation!

Relationships After Kids

For those of you that haven't had kids just yet; I'm sorry to say, but your relationship will be over when the little one(s) emerge. There's not much more to it…

Relationships After Kids (Part 2)

Ok, sorry … my little joke.

Yes, of course relationships continue after kids begin arriving, but let's just say that things … umm; will change. One could argue that change is inevitable, regardless of whether or not children enter the equation. However, kids present certain challenges to the further development and/or maintenance of a romantic partnership. These challenges cannot be fully appreciated (ha ha) until you're on the battlefield. This is why I get frustrated with childless people who say, 'well, you chose to have kids', when I vent about the joys of parenthood.

One moment you're snuggling together in bed all day, eating takeout and snoozing. You binge on chocolate and mainline Netflix shows. There is no impediment to intimacy. You can repeat the process all weekend … it's just divine. The next moment you're scratching your head and looking at this partner in hedonism and wondering how you went from all that fun stuff to becoming business associates running a day care centre. Congratulations; you're a parent!

All joking aside, in between those moments of exhausted bewilderment, you'll both look at what has hijacked your bed full of Dorito crumbs and Lindt wrappers, and lovingly marvel at what you've created. Such is parenthood; living at emotional extremes day to day, moment to moment. You've exchanged weekends lounging in bed for the best hugs in the universe; and it's every bit worth it. Worth it; yes … easy; no.

My wife and I have often wondered how kids relentlessly try to destroy (albeit unconsciously) the very thing they depend on for their survival. I mean, sure, kids can handle living in a divorce situation, spending weekends with their dad, and the week with their mom; or whatever the arrangement might be. But what they really want is a happy, two-parent household, right? However, with every sleepless night and the exhausting litany of needs, kids unknowingly, innocently, erode the very thing they want.

The above situation is what has led innumerable couples to marriage counselling and/or the divorce courts. So, how do you nurture a healthy, fun relationship with your partner and also raise those kids properly? Sorry; I have no idea. And even if I had the magic formula, I'm not qualified to dispense such advice in any official capacity and needless to say; each family is different. There are myriad variables that go into keeping a relationship vibrant and exciting even without the kid angle, so of course the challenges grow exponentially when little ones are added to the mix.

Hey, maybe you're among the lucky ones that have kids and a super-solid relationship without many issues, past or present. However, most parents struggle at one time or another. I mean, one of the most essential requirements for a healthy relationship is spending time together and communicating. However, there's usually a kid interrupting every conversation. By the time the children are down for the night, parents' usually have no energy for this thing called a relationship. All they can do is zombie out on their phones.

Other kid-related stresses that significantly affect relationships revolve around finances. Food bills, clothing, braces, birthdays and Christmas, etc. You name it; if it involves kids, it costs money. How to most effectively spend the money that the family does have is a major hot button with parents. It's pretty overwhelming at times, right? It's pretty overwhelming every day, right?

Once again, I have no answers. I'm just illuminating general issues ... the ones my relationship has, and yours might have, too. All we can do is take it day by day and keep laughing. However, with or without kids, relationships evolve from the infatuation stage to something else. That something else can be embraced or shunned, but it seems to be hastened by the presence of children. Little ones are the ultimate relationship testers.

When I worked full time, Louise and I used to take the train into the city together. We'd have an hour each way to hang out and chat without interruptions. Can you believe it; no kids talking over us! However, now that I'm home with our three daughters, the opportunities for quality time together have reduced drastically. By the time she walks in the door, I'm fried mentally, and the children have their reign until it's bedtime. When they are in bed and actually stay there, mom and dad are toast.

Of course, this doesn't mean that relationships are doomed once kids arrive, but a concerted effort is required to feed that which created those kids in the first place. It's hard work on top of hard work and it's worth it. But you just have to laugh when you're sitting on the couch with your partner, trying to have a conversation and this little person squishes their way between you or dives onto your laps from the coffee table. That's a double scoop of what the fu*k! Oh well…

So, once again, how do you keep a relationship thriving amid the maelstrom of raising children? I have no idea; I'm not qualified to give professional advice on such matters. Yes, I know I already said that. The kids have fried my brain. Is yours fried yet? I now forget things like where the car is parked and call the children by the wrong names. I repeat myself like my parents did, and it's scary. This is your brain on drugs. This is your brain on kids … pretty much the same but without the euphoria; or so I've heard.

My relationship isn't perfect. However, I'd recommend that you keep talking to your partner. Get off the phone and talk; and do other stuff as often as possible. That other 'stuff' will keep you connected mentally and emotionally which, in my humble opinion, is absolutely critical to parent happiness in the home. If you're not getting along or just barely tolerating each other, you won't be able to be supportive. Without mutual support, you'll just fight and then everything crumbles from there.

If you are fortunate enough to be able to drop the kids at a grandparent's house or with some other trustworthy family member, do it as often as possible. Go for a date night or stay at a hotel if you can. I know that orchestrating such activities can be tiring, but your relationship (and indirectly your children) needs it. Louise and I don't have this option; and as many of you know, it's super-difficult on a relationship without the support of extended family. We might move back to America just for the free babysitting!

I'll tell you a story about the last time we had a night away. It was my birthday and we stayed up the road from our house; just to be nearby in case the babysitter needed us. It was a cute Tudor style bed and breakfast. Each room had a theme. Ours was Victorian England or something. We were going to party. We had wine and snacks, etc. But then we just collapsed in bed, exhausted. Sound familiar?

Relationships After Kids (Part 2)

Louise finally had a chance to watch Star Trek, uninterrupted. I got pissed because I don't really care for the new Star Trek and didn't want to cause a fight, so I went all quiet and fell asleep. I know, very juvenile. Anyway, there was no party because of the aforementioned exhaustion and also, I didn't want to get drunk and spill red wine on those nice rugs. Ironically, the best part of the stay was when we woke up. I know what you're thinking, but no.

Afterwards, we both agreed that the best part was the morning after. This is because we got to watch a Netflix show with coffee ... alone! Wait, say that again ... alone! There were no kids talking over the show or bouncing on the bed or fighting in the next room. Whoa! Not possible! Initially, we had a bit of the old PTPD (Post Traumatic Parenting Disorder) where we were expecting kid-chaos any moment, but it didn't happen. Wow; coffee in bed with a decent show. That is what every relationship needs. Or at least the equivalent in your own personal universe.

Just do your best. Kids will likely erase the infatuation high of your relationship (if it isn't gone already) and you've got to evolve with it as joyfully as possible. Remember ... they are watching; always watching, listening, and absorbing. How you interact with your partner is forming their childhood memories and influencing what types of people they will be drawn to as adults. I hope this doesn't sound preachy; I just don't know how else to put it. Even during the rough patches, try to make the best of it.

Isolation and Sense of Identity

This is, by far, the hardest part for me as a home-parent. I recently did a Twitter poll and although the response wasn't huge, isolation was also the most challenging for other SAHP's. The sense of identity part is interconnected, as isolation breeds an inordinate amount of self-analysis. Scary stuff indeed. Without an active world around to reflect us back at ourselves, we can become rather eccentric. Weird becomes our norm and we start getting quizzical looks while chattering away during rare instances of adult interaction.

When the kids are at school or napping, it's just you and four walls. People that work full time and haven't done the SAHP job almost

The Hardest Job I've Ever Had - Stay at Home Dad

always say they'd jump at the chance to be home with all of that 'free' time. They say that they wouldn't have to deal with idiot colleagues and office politics, etc. I was that person, too. Don't get me wrong; as hard as it is, I wouldn't trade this time with my children for anything. But now I see the other side of the coin.

A stay-at-home parent has no workmates; at least in the traditional sense. They have nobody in the adjacent cubicle to safely rant to about something going on in their personal lives. They don't have a 'piss and moan club'. Without this type of support mechanism, repressed emotions such as frustration and anger can fester and create a host of physical and emotional problems as well as addictions.

The idea of staying at home with the kids and not being accountable to an adult supervisor is very appealing from a conceptual perspective. However, a baby-boss can be the most brutal of taskmasters ... and that's a boss you can't quit. Whether or not you knew who you were before your life as a SAHP, all sense of identity is stripped away into the vortex of an empty, yet paradoxically very full house. The frightening part is not knowing if you'll ever be 'you' again and if that person will be recognizable in the mirror. This job transforms

Isolation and Sense of Identity

you. The metamorphosis may or may not be overt, but rest assured, the person you were before kids will seem like they're from an alternate universe. The isolation, stress, and also love for your children are powerful catalysts for change.

Whether or not you want to revive the person you were before kids, or completely reinvent yourself, I think it's imperative that you have something just for you. Maybe it's running a small business, or working a part-time job, or perhaps an interesting hobby that makes you feel joy. If you're not already doing something like this, please take the first steps. Do it for you, and for your family. Isolation does strange things to the mind.

If you feel depressed, and the idea of doing anything except the bare minimum is inconceivable because your kids are exhausting, you're not alone. My first few months at home were a shocker. I couldn't get much more accomplished beyond feeding them, dressing them, and driving them around. Oh; and a lot of yelling. Just like any new job, and I think even more so with this one, it takes at least six months to settle into it. At the time of this writing, I'm coming up on a year and still struggle daily.

When you're alone or with kids most of the time, your intellectual side starves. Well, at least mine did. I longed for a proper, two-way conversation but nobody was ever around. On the flipside, this loneliness can make you self-isolate against your instincts. It's such a strange dynamic, and when you're in the middle of it, you feel nuts. You desperately want to talk to people, so you run away from them? Huh? It makes no sense.

This reminds me of a time after I had completed over two months of school holidays with the kids. Classes were finally back in session and I was dropping them off when some of the other parents said hi and wanted to engage. I freaked and hurried away. During the vacation period, I was going nuts and whining a lot on Parent Twitter about how isolated I felt. On the surface, it made no sense to run away from those other adults. Have you ever felt lonely, yet simultaneously recoiled when given the opportunity to interact?

This was a real eye-opener for me; observing my own contradictory behaviour from the outside. I have chalked this up to some weird form of the Stockholm Syndrome, where my captor is isolation itself. As a SAHP, I've become acutely aware of how powerfully isolation can affect the mind and that we are indeed social creatures. My big-man ego is embarrassed to admit it, but I really do crave a

Isolation and Sense of Identity

certain amount of daily social contact to keep my sanity.

The mental health community needs to come up with a snazzy clinical term for this particular strain of isolation disorder. It feels like being locked in a hotel room for twenty years with the cartoon channel playing continuously. It's impossible to properly convey this with mere words; one has to experience it to fully understand. If you're in the club, you'll know what I mean. If you're on your way to the club (planning for or currently expecting kids), God help you. Just kidding ... sort of.

SAHP's must deal with the (additional) mental challenges of stuff that bubbles up from the unconscious. The parts of our psyches that are ordinarily subdued by the buzz and distractions of regular jobs emerge while we're alone at home and they demand attention. They won't leave us alone until we engage with them and that can be pretty scary. Home-parents are always busy, but this type of 'isolated busy' won't easily keep the denizens of our mental abyss at bay.

Another thing that intensifies the effects of isolation is the monotony involved with being a SAHP. I'm definitely a creature of habit and although I simultaneously complain about and crave routine; this kind of repetition is very challenging mentally. After years of watching spy movies and thinking that leaving someone all alone in a room for long periods of time wouldn't compel them to divulge state secrets, I now understand. The only problem is that when my wife gets home in the evening, she often tunes out my state secrets because I'm so hyper-excited to talk to an adult that it's overwhelming for her.

The monotony starts first thing in the morning. Emptying the dishwasher and prepping counter space for breakfast and lunch-making triggers irritation as my desire for something new and exciting is once again not satisfied. However, I do try to make the kids' food with as much love and attention to detail as possible. The sandwich artist within gets to shine. That is, until the Witching Hour when my 'food art' comes back uneaten and/or mushed into the sides of lunchboxes … oh well.

This type of mind-numbing routine continues throughout the day. It includes endless dishwasher duty, laundry, toy clean-up, vacuuming, trash bag removal, counter wiping, and my personal favourite, toilet paper roll disposal. This is nothing new to SAHP's; you guys know the drill. It's boring, but these tasks are so very important for the maintenance and development of our spawn. This is what I tell myself on the good days. On the other days, I just pound carbs and coffee to get through it all.

In a strange way, this endless repetition creates a sort of trance state where our minds and bodies are disconnected as we observe ourselves completing the daily chores from a distance. The mind wanders to a more pleasurable locale as the body does what is necessary, yet oh-so unfulfilling. Is this a survival mechanism with the unfortunate side effect of being disembodied? Feeling numb to get through the moment is of course dangerous in the long term. We know we should keep ourselves stimulated with other, more engaging activities but there is little extra time and we're always so exhausted, right?

It gets to the point where what you contribute becomes invisible to the rest of the family. They get used to everything that you do and the only time you get any feedback is when your standard drops below the norm. Then you get an indirect vibe that feels like they think you're getting lazy and not doing your 'job' which is of course (to them) unacceptable. Well, that's how it feels to me, at least. I know I might sound a bit paranoid and nutty but that's what being home alone all the time can do to you.

This is the most thankless job in the universe; which is so ironic because without the next generation, there is no future. That may seem dramatic, but it's true. To people who work regular jobs, I'm a complainer. I sound like a lucky guy who is just whining and doesn't know how 'easy' he has it. However, to SAHP's, I'm speaking the truth, right? Everything is upside-down; priorities are in the wrong place. How did all of this happen? Surely there was a time in history when parenting was officially accepted as the most important duty?

I'm generalizing here as I am sure there are spouses and kids that do thank the SAHP's who look after them but overall, there isn't enough recognition. Regular jobs have a salary (receiving a weekly/biweekly check feels great) bonuses, and programmes like 'employee of the month', etc. Even those who profess not to be motivated by such things (money aside) surely feel good when they are recognized in these various ways. It must put a bit of wind in their sails, right? However, the power of a sincere thank you cannot be underestimated.

It can take many years for someone to truly appreciate what their parents did for them. Quite often, people only 'get it' when they become parents themselves, and that's certainly understandable. However, by and large, the daily struggles of a SAHP are hidden in plain sight. To other adults, we have the dream job; to our kids, we're vending machines of food, hugs, and clean clothes. Maybe the repetition itself makes us invisible?

All complaining aside; I truly believe that we as parents are given the gift of being able to care for another life (or lives). We shouldn't really expect appreciation. However, SAHP's are definitely not thanked as often as they should be for the hard work and love they put into their households.

Discipline and Guilt

Discipline is the biggest issue in our house. Guilt quite often follows, but I'll get to that in a moment. We have rules and steps of the disciplinary process posted on the wall for the kids to see but as I'm sure you know, it's not always that easy. Should there be another warning before a time-out? Do we have the energy to follow through? One parent countermands the other in front of the kids, etc. Children are not machines; what worked last week to keep them in line is suddenly useless.

I look at the home as a 'reality theatre' of sorts. It's a place to teach kids how to behave properly with the safety net of a loving environment where they'll get an explanation around cause and effect. If we let them slide on things because we love them too much, are too exhausted to follow through, or think they'll 'figure it out' our kids will likely turn into jerks (or worse ... a**holes!) as adults. As hard as it is, we do them a disservice when misbehaviour isn't properly dealt with.

On the flipside, I find it so very painful to discipline my kids. I'm not talking about being too exhausted to follow through, but rather seeing them cry when they have to go in the time-out corner. Yes, I'm sure it's a manipulative tactic at times, but it rips my guts out to hear them whimper. I feel their pain physically; they are my little babies. Maybe they can just live at home forever, so I don't have to endure the emotional pain of teaching them boundaries? No such luck; it has to be done.

Our system is pretty standard; one minute in the time-out corner according to age. It does work, but the hard part is consistent follow-through. The kids always know when we're tired and/or distracted and thus apt to give extra warnings. Once they see that there is wiggle-room, they gamble like they're in Vegas ... and they usually win! Why? We love them and can't stand seeing them upset. Or, we blame ourselves for the bad behaviour and rationalize that it's not entirely their fault. After all, they learn everything from us, right? Shouldn't the bad parents be punished? It's really hard, isn't it?

I'm certainly no expert. You might use variations on this, or perhaps something completely different. With our eldest daughter, being sent to bed early or taking screen time away works too. However, it would be nice if kids just followed directives implicitly after the first infraction. Ok; I sound like a drill sergeant, but it's just maddening that they can't listen and remember. Sure, they hear us, but the listening somehow gets lost in translation. As I often frustratedly exclaim after they shrug me off for the umpteenth time; ponies and rainbows are obviously more interesting!

Ponies and rainbows take precedence in kids' minds. This is a scientific fact. We probably sound just like the adults on Charlie Brown to them. You know; on the Snoopy cartoon when the parents and teachers talk, and it comes out as gibberish? That's how I deal with being ignored; just chalk it up to the old Charlie Brown effect. Yes, of course I'm deluding myself. They are aware of what we're saying but also know they can get away with a lot and push those boundaries. I wonder how much of this insubordination is fully conscious, though. I guess it depends on age and individual level of awareness, etc.

However, they are not adults yet. Their minds are still developing. Well, that's what I have to consistently remind myself of because anger and frustration in the moment usually override logic. I know, this is nothing new to most parents, but I suspect it's nice to hear from someone else. Because our kids are so connected to us, I really think it's extra difficult because it feels like we're disciplining ourselves, if that makes sense?

We've also had to change our time-out location several times as the kids have found ways to make their sentence in the naughty corner more bearable. They will stretch out on the floor and watch TV when we're not looking, or smuggle in a little toy to keep them occupied, etc. As most of you probably know, their bedroom is not a good location for isolation punishment. They just play or look at a picture book. So, as the different locations' shortcomings have emerged, we've changed them. Of course, it all depends on the layout of your home and what area is most effective.

How kids behave alone with the SAHP is often completely different when the other parent arrives home from work. Before proceeding, I don't want those who have nannies or are single parents to feel as though I'm ignoring them. I'm just focusing on what I'm going through at the moment as it's fresh in my mind. For the record, I grew up in a single-parent home and as previously mentioned, my wife and I have been on the nanny-go-round.

Ok; getting back to kids' behaviour with the SAHP, versus when the other parent walks in the door. Louise and I have recently clashed over our kids' unruliness and her assumption that I'm not sticking to the disciplinary system when she's at work. However, while the children do act up occasionally when she's not there, I certainly put them in time-out when it's necessary. What she doesn't realize is that they always, always go bonkers as soon as she gets home.

Aside from fighting over food in the car right after school, or later at home over which cartoon to watch, it's pretty routine. That doesn't mean they don't nag me senseless with requests for snacks, butt-wipes, Band Aids for non-existent injuries, or to go on a safari for a missing toy, etc. it just means that there is generally no extreme behaviour warranting time-outs. Sure; it does happen but I'm always right on it. However, when mom gets home, they do anything they can to get her undivided attention.

This includes negative attention through acting up.

By the time our kids are fed and ready for bed, Louise and I are usually exhausted and snappy; with the children and with each other. Sound familiar? Since joining Parent Twitter (to be discussed at length in the next chapter), I've found that this is rather common. Although I'm not taking joy in other parents' struggles, it's comforting to know that we're not alone.

One time, I tried to send a profanity-laced message to Louise about Zoe having a meltdown. Unfortunately, it went to Emily's friend's mom as we'd recently texted to arrange a playdate. She immediately knew she wasn't the intended recipient and thought it was hilarious, but also comforting in the same way I just mentioned above. After we cleared things up, she said it sounded so much like her house. She then came back to me with this phrase, which rang very true. 'Raising little people is so damn hard!'

Getting back to discipline; a strange thing I've noticed is a sort of pride that arises when my kids are rebellious or act up in a righteous way. Part of me knows they need a reprimand, and part of me smiles inwardly and is glad they're standing up for what they think is right; regardless of the consequences. How can we

Discipline and Guilt

not secretly cheer on a little version of ourselves as they challenge the system?

Of course, this can get out of hand if not kept in check. Parents must decide how much controlled, intelligent rebellion to foster in their kids. I like to give mine a framework for how to operate within 'the system', so that it doesn't wear them down before they've built up some resistance to the Matrix. In my humble parenting opinion, too much rebellion training too soon makes one a target and can sometimes have the opposite effect.

But then again, I suspect that a good portion of a child's tendency to buck the system might very well be unconscious, learned behaviour. They watch us and they mimic, simple as that. Maybe in the end, we've all turned into our parents and our kids will inevitably turn into us. Are you ok with that? Do we even have an option? It's certainly debatable from both sides, with many variables to consider.

Like most parents, I want my kids to get to the point where they think about the potential consequences before acting on rule-breaking impulses. Of course, it's not that easy but having a goal with discipline is important. Sometimes children keep breaking rules and you start worrying that your disciplinary system is a failure. Do you keep doing the same thing or start watching Super Nanny videos on YouTube for help?

Kids thrive on routine and consistency so I wouldn't recommend changing things too often or drastically. To be fair; what if you were the child and sometimes, you're in the naughty corner after one warning, then the next time no warnings, or maybe three? What kind of message does that send? On the parent end of things, it's usually about time and energy. Do we have the time to implement discipline or will we be late (yet again) for stopping everything for a time-out? Even more problematic is the oomph required to follow through with punishment when we're perpetually exhausted and eat most meals standing up. If you sit, you'll likely be standing again in two seconds anyway, right?

Regardless; it's extremely challenging to be consistent with a disciplinary regimen. Plus; kids are always expanding intellectually, and as previously mentioned, what worked to keep them on the straight and narrow yesterday can be an utter failure today. Yes; it's the hardest job in the universe. That's it! Get your butt in time-out!

If there's one thing that's universal in parenting (aside from Go the Fu*k to Sleep!) it's guilt. From day one, you're feeling guilt, right?

Discipline and Guilt

They should emerge from the womb with a little guilt pamphlet. A tiny, laminated introduction to your new and constant companions going forward. By companions, I mean the kid and the guilt. In the very beginning, when they're little and can't pick up on it yet, it's just you and your guilt. However, after they weaponize your guilt, that's when the real challenge begins. What do I mean by weaponize? If you don't know already, read on and you'll see.

Parental guilt after disciplining a child is certainly common and in many cases it's automatic. However, the guilt train doesn't stop there; at least for me. Before proceeding, I just wanted to let you know that in situations with people other than my kids, guilt doesn't rule me. People love to drop guilt trips and manipulate with it and that just pisses me off. If someone tries to guilt me, I call them out immediately.

However; I'm a sucker for my kids and feel guilty about a lot of stuff. That doesn't mean I let it totally control me but it's definitely an area I need to work on. I'm also aware that my kids pick up on my guilt reactions and this will likely factor into how they relate with others going forward. Needless to say, this isn't good so I'm really trying to eradicate the negative side of guilt as it can become quite poisonous. However, there are certain things that always give me a pang of it despite the fact that I know I'm doing my best as a parent and love my kids to the moon and back.

Dropping them off at school doesn't make me feel so much guilty as uncomfortably nostalgic; or am I rationalizing? I know they need an education and socialization, so school is necessary. Yes; I'm aware that many chose to home-school, and I certainly don't pass judgement either way … to each their own. I don't want to open a can of worms with that subject as we all have different viewpoints and personal situations, etc.

But the school environment (the sounds and smells) evokes foggy childhood memories. My subconscious stirs as I travel decades into the past, to a place where I felt scared and alone in the classroom. I wanted to go home, and I project that onto my kids and assume they are feeling the same things. They're probably not. Emily, my five-year-old, loves going to school. Beth, who's thirteen, says school is boring but that's standard for her age. I can tell that she likes it. It's obvious they need the stimulation and opportunity to form relationships outside the home with kids their own age.

Day care is much harder for me, though. Zoe still goes and I always feel guilty for leaving her there. I know that she also needs socialization as she will be at big-girl school with her sisters next year. She absolutely loves going to play with the other kids and definitely needs the stimulation as she gets very bored at home and then causes trouble. The staff at her day care are great, too.

That still doesn't stop me from feeling guilty. I should be hanging out with her as much as possible, right? She isn't at day care as long as the older girls are at school, but I feel like a bad parent for leaving her there at all. As previously mentioned, she's got a half-day on Tuesdays and is completely off on Wednesdays which is our special time together. We go to parent-assisted gymnastics and then afterwards eat pistachios and watch cartoons. And sometimes, she goes down for a short nap and I get one too! However, I definitely need the time when she is at day care for getting stuff done and for me-time; yet I still feel guilty. Why?

But the guilt train just keeps on chugging along. You have days when you just don't want to be a parent, right? You wake up and you can barely fathom how you're going to get just you through the day, let alone several kids. On these mornings I can barely motivate myself to get dressed and brush my teeth, so how am I going to get these little people to do such things when they're highly resistant to them, even in good moods?

I just want to drop them off at a different house. Why can't I sometimes leave them with another adult who will do the feeding and dressing, etc? Why can't someone else trudge through the deep mud, the gale force winds, and the underwater slog of the morning routine? Yes; that is what it usually feels like. But there are no sick days in the life of a SAHP. You have to do it, rain or shine. And I do get it done; yet the guilt over sometimes not wanting to is always there.

Another place where guilt surfaces for me is when I chose to do my own thing such as writing or marketing my books. I do spend time with the kids, but as previously mentioned, I definitely need some degree of creative nourishment or I'll become depressed and irritable. They get so happy when I spend time doing a puzzle with them or even just sitting and watching a cartoon. I'd like to do that more often but if I don't carve out some daily time for myself, things go downhill fast, mentally. It's always a struggle to find balance in this area.

Giving them another fifteen minutes or so of placating tablet time when I'm in the middle of cooking or just plain exhausted is something I feel bad about too. Part of me knows that my kids have been born into a world of technology and they need to understand it and learn their way around it. However, it's also pretty obvious that too much isn't good for them. In many ways, it's similar to candy in that they nag you for it and it makes them happy, but you know there are side effects.

On the subject of food; I think our diet is very healthy and balanced overall, but sometimes I feel bad for throwing a packet of chips at them instead of chopping up apples or carrot sticks. They are such nags that you just can't handle the incessant badgering while you're doing the peeling and cutting, so whatever requires no preparation is sometimes the only viable option. Am I making excuses? I just don't know.

That being said, kids definitely have no patience whatsoever. If you're a parent, you already knew that! When they have to pee, it's NOW. When they're hungry, it's NOW. Make them wait and they'll make you pay ... dearly. But youngsters with no 'patience training' become jerky adults. It's so hard; isn't it?

Playdates are of course great for children but also for parents. Mustering the social energy for them can be such a challenge, though. I feel guilty for cancelling at the last minute. The kids are so disappointed and cannot understand why daddy just isn't able to face anyone right now. However, I've been cancelled on so often that I realized the other parents were likely experiencing the same issues. Or, there's something wrong with me? Oh well; I can't be entirely sure.

But after comparing notes with other moms and dads during the school run and on playdates that did happen as scheduled, I've found that we all cancel for this reason. Once again, SAHP isolation creates the paradox of seeking adult interaction while receding into your turtle shell when it's time to play. Unfortunately, this affects the kids as well because they miss out on socializing with other children. I suppose that the parent gets worn out one way or the other. Why?

Right after cancelling a playdate to avoid dealing with other adults, your kids drive you nuts, and you wish you had gotten them out the door for some energy-burning fun. But alas, it's too late. You promise yourself not to cancel again but chances are that you will. It's a tough choice … stay in the house and be driven loony by your own creatures or put on the uncomfortable playdate social mask? I feel guilty because I know it's best for my kids to get out there.

Discipline and Guilt

When the stress is overwhelming, I occasionally think that I don't like this job and I'm just not cut out for it. Then I feel terribly guilty because I associate not 'liking' the job with not loving my kids which is of course ridiculous. However, being a SAHP isn't what I thought it would be. I'm pretty much a domestic that happens to work in the same home my children live in. Why shouldn't I be allowed to dislike being an unappreciated butler? I'm always grumbling that I'm just a servant, waiting for the next dish to scrape or basket of dirty laundry to wash. Am I doing something wrong? Is there a trick to making this the fun job I thought it would be?

I also feel guilty for complaining about my kids in general. But while being a parent is wonderful and I sincerely appreciate it, the experience is often traumatic. Without the stress release valve of complaining, I'd go bonkers. I would prefer that my children don't read this book until becoming parents themselves as they might think I'm a real a**hole for whining so much and that I don't love them. Of course, that's as far from the truth as possible. However, without their own parenting experiences, they just wouldn't understand.

Parent Twitter

Following on from all of that complaining and guilt in the previous chapter; I have found a wonderful outlet! Picture this … or maybe not. It's eight thirty in the morning and your kids are melting down. One tantrum has spread like a wildfire and the whole place has gone mad. You were so close to getting out the door on time and now there's no way that will happen. Your spouse, the person who gets to talk to other adults, has already left for work. What to do? Carbs? Alcohol? Lock yourself in the bathroom and cry? Run away? No … better yet, lock yourself in the bathroom and compose a mayday Tweet. This brief and therapeutic exercise has saved my sanity more times than I can count.

The mayday Tweet I sent out went to all of my friends on Parent Twitter. This online subcommunity has been a godsend. What started out as a marketing tool has turned into an amazing support network for my journey as a SAHP. The internet really is the perfect way for busy, lonely, and (paradoxically) reclusive home-parents to connect. We long for some sort of intellectual stimulus and camaraderie but usually don't feel up to dealing with people face-to-face.

When I worked in an office, small exchanges with co-workers were a sort of social sustenance that I didn't recognize as such until I was cooped up in the house with dishes, laundry, and crumbs on the rug. I didn't particularly care for some of them, but their absence has certainly illuminated the psychological value they provided. Who would have thought that people you have little or nothing in common with, or even personalities that were like claws on a chalkboard, could make you happy? Or perhaps the better way to describe it would be that they could keep you from being depressed and lonely.

SAHP life often creates the desire for a quick exchange with someone who understands; or will at least nod blankly when you vent your frustrations. Whether it's the monotony and isolation, or the brain damage following a kid's meltdown, the home-parent's need for immediate support usually cannot be met. This is where Parent Twitter comes to the rescue. People who get it, right inside your phone! How do they all fit in there?

I cannot tell you how satisfying a quick break to craft an SOS Tweet can be when you're on the edge of madness. Like a more reliable version of the age-old message in a bottle, your Tweet is riding the interwebs on its way to sympathetic eyes and brains. A Like and/or reply can open the valve of your emotional pressure cooker, helping you back away from the cliff's edge. Away from the cliff and back to the dishes ... oh well.

With my previous books, I'd Tweet a sentence or two each day during the writing process. These Tweets were meant to keep potential readers engaged and find new folks that might be interested in the book when it came out. This marketing approach takes time, but it's the only way to build relationships with people who are interested in what you're writing about. After launching a book, I'd Tweet links to it on Amazon, reviews as they came in, and other promotional stuff to keep sales going. A self-published author doesn't make much, but it's nice to help put food on the table doing what you love.

However, with Parent Twitter, I quickly noticed that I was Tweeting for support to keep my sanity. This was (and still is) less about book sales and more about navigating the Cape Horn of parenthood ... being a SAHP! As you well-know, parenting isn't a curiosity or side interest. With kids, you're all-in for a long, long time so whatever helpful info I came across on Twitter, it was more about survival than entertainment. I was so very happy to be working towards completing a book that might in some way be useful to fellow parents. As I let them know about it on social media, their responses and engagement were keeping my psyche from crumbling around me as the loneliness and monotony chipped away at my soul. I don't care if that sounds dramatic ... it's really how I felt.

Being a parent is like being in a special club where you don't have to know all of the other members personally. It's a journey that we all share, and being in the trenches with the poop, tantrums, and sleepless nights is something that people without kids will never get. The childless aunt or uncle that babysits your little balls of hyperkinetic energy while you and hubby catch a movie, only gets a microdose of parenthood.

While we do appreciate their support, a few hours won't do the job justice. A babysitter might leave your house slightly dizzy and bewildered but think, 'it's not so bad, I could do that.' However, we as parents know that the cumulative effect is what drives us mad. Like the drip drip of water torture, the repetition of kid chaos is the hardest part. And that's why Parent Twitter is so special to me. When my wife isn't around to lean on, those cyber friends are the ones who get it … and they're awesome!

The effects of parenting have created some delightfully interesting characters. If you don't have a Twitter account, sign up and check it out. The great thing about Twitter is that you can be someone else. You aren't required to use your real name. Go ahead, be 'Sleepless Mom' or 'Grumpy Dad' or 'Stressed Out in Seattle'. Be whatever you feel best describes the part of you that wants to attract similar types of Twitter friends. Do a search for things like #momlife, #SAHP, #parenthood, etc. Those hashtags will give you lists of people to follow. It's medicine for a parent's frayed nerves. It's like a glass of wine when you can't have one until after the school run.

I'll give you some examples of when Parent Twitter came to the rescue. I've been on the couch many times with tantrum-induced migraines and sent SOS Tweets hoping to find quick, genuine support to get me through the remainder of the Witching Hour. Sure enough, responses arrived like aspirin kicking in. I knew I wasn't alone. That sympathetic engagement got me off the couch and back into the kitchen and laundry room to finish the afternoon drudgery. Thanks everyone!

I've also got some fond memories of being in the car before kamikaze grocery store missions with three kids. As much as I strongly advise (as strongly as possible ... like really, really, really strongly) not bringing kids food shopping, sometimes it has to happen. So anyway, just before heading over Niagara Falls in a shopping cart, I'd Tweet to my parent friends how scared I was. This would give me enough courage to survive the brain trauma to come.

Afterwards in the car, to begin the healing process, I'd check my responses. I heard from supportive (and often hilarious) parents who knew what it was like to endure what I'd just gone through. As much as social media and phones are keeping us from being present in 'real life', they do have their benefits in certain situations. Before heading home, I'd Tweet back any highlights from the grocery store visit. The circle was now complete. Cyber camaraderie to the rescue!

Parent Twitter comes in handy after the school run, too. During the morning madness, there's usually something to share; some sort of occurrence that only a fellow kid wrangler can appreciate. In the old days, you'd have to keep these experiential gems to yourself until dinnertime, but not anymore. A current favourite is Tweeting about the dreadful treatment I receive from the school office staff when we're late (which is fairly often). Ok; it's not dreadful, but more like chilly.

When we're tardy, we usually arrive anywhere from five to thirty minutes after the second bell. I'm often frantic and get a bit wacky when all hyped up and stressed out, so I try some jokes to pad the vibe of disappointment coming from across the school reception desk. In particular, my 'bigfoot came for breakfast' excuse really fell flat. I didn't get a single smile, and Beth was mortified. So, afterwards I ranted about this on Twitter and felt much better. Aside from hearing that other late parents also receive this kind of treatment, I was given some great advice on how to build a better relationship with the school office staff.

I've also Tweeted about having my super-organized kitchen thrown into chaos on the weekends due to my wife being home. I didn't receive much sympathy there. I was told to appreciate the extra help and chill out, which is exactly what I did. In general, every time I'm overwhelmed with parenting stress, I chirp and Tweet my frustrations away ... its wonderful!

Parent Twitter is an unofficial subgroup, but then there are more subgroups within the main subgroup. For instance (and I'm heavily generalizing); there are the parents that swear a lot and talk about guzzling wine during the Witching Hour. Then there are the home-schooling moms and dads, singles, dirty joke tellers, and of course those wonderful Canadians. There are tons more; have a look. I don't judge any of them. They're all great because we're all in it together; chatting about the daily joys and struggles that come with being parents. It's so very interesting if you have kids, and I suspect so very uninteresting if you don't.

What's discussed at this online piss and moan club? Anything from poopy diapers to debates over how much screen time is healthy, getting kids to fall asleep at night, babysitters, endless housework, and everything in-between. There are quite a few lonely and depressed SAHP's out there and that was the hardest thing for me; especially at the beginning. Participating in talks about the inner world of a home-parent are my personal favourites. Rest assured, there's something for everyone in this cyber city for moms and dads ... check it out!

A bittersweet irony of parenting youngsters is that it's so exhausting we often want them to grow up just a little bit and be more self-sufficient before we lose our minds. They drip-feed cuteness and cuddles as a sort of primal defence mechanism to keep us washing their clothes and wiping their bums. Years from now, they will periodically return home to steal toilet paper and canned goods to stock their apartments. Did you ever do that?

Yes, they will be gone someday and then the house will really be empty. Not just from nine to three, but all the time. So, how do we enjoy their younger years while keeping our sanity? Right now, they actually want to hang out with us and think we're cool. It won't last long, though. Parenting is the best job we'll ever have and we must enjoy it while we can

.

The Best Job I've Ever Had

This might not be the longest chapter but it's certainly the most important. Sure; I've blathered on throughout the book complaining about my kids and how hard it is being a parent. It's all true, but still, I love them to the moon and back and want to get the most out of this brief time with them. Soon they'll be grown up and independent. I'm worried about this.

As I type, it's very early in the morning and I hear one of the kids stir in bed. I freeze with a mixture of parental concern and frustration. 'Damn, I'm getting up at the crack of dawn to write this book about you little people and you're threatening to steal my creative time with an early wake-up?' Sounds terrible, doesn't it? Am I a self-centred egomaniac? Most parents would say no; they'd understand. But they'd also understand why I feel bad for getting irritated at the thought of my kids disturbing this special me-time.

After all, being a SAHP is about the children; or at least it should be. I'm very fortunate to have this opportunity during such an important stage in their lives. And they love spending time with me; I'm a rock star! I don't embarrass them (except for Beth) and get a hug and kiss at school drop-off and pick-up. However, writing this book, putting these daily parenting challenges into words, is keeping me sane.

On Parent Twitter I often come across rants from overwhelmed moms and dads about barely getting through the day and trying to make the most of the odd occasion when they can drop the little ones off at grandma's house or get a sitter. One couple even hilariously calculated how much kid-free activity they could get in before collecting their sugared-up bundles of joy. Because let's face it, even if you do get a break, the kids will likely be difficult afterwards. Grandparents spoil with gifts and candy. Babysitters usually don't know all the house rules and let them get away with stuff. Ok; I'm getting off point ... see what kid brain does to you!

Anyway, these Twitter threads often have a comment or two from empty nesters that chime in with something like, 'they'll be gone in the blink of an eye and you'll miss them', etc. This used to irritate me because as a stressed out SAHP of three kids, someone who no longer has to officiate endless screaming and scratching fights over two identical toys or who's got more Cheetos has no right to tell me to enjoy it while I can; agreed? Do these people have amnesia? I really think they block it all out.

Lately though, I've considered the flipside. Perhaps those empty nester amnesiacs are onto something. I can actually see ahead to the day when my little buddies are off in their teenaged worlds with social groups and interests that take precedence over mom and dad. Just a short time later, they'll be out of the house and I'll be chasing them for attention. Sure, kids come back to 'borrow' money and to sneak food from the pantry, but by then parents take a permanent back seat to their exciting young adult lives. So yes; I need to make the most of this precious time. But how?

I've given quite a bit of thought as to how I react when I get an e-mail from my parents trying to schedule a video call. I have been living abroad for eight years now and have only seen them in person once during that time. I'm embarrassed to admit that I occasionally get irritated when they want to catch up with me for an hour and see how big their grandchildren are getting. Heck, we only chat once a month so it's not that big of an imposition. I must sound like a selfish, ungrateful a jerk. After all, my parents raised me and have occasionally bailed me out of financial trouble as an adult. I shouldn't be reacting this way when they just want to say hello.

The most frightening part of this is that my own little ones might someday react in the same manner to my requests for attention. Parent Twitter friends have reassured me that as long as I give them all the love and attention I can, they will treat me the same way after beginning their adult lives. I really hope so. I think I'll especially enjoy my kids' company when they're able to have philosophical conversations and reflect on their experiences and the world around them. Right now, though, at their current age, the day-to-day stuff is hard. I feel guilty for not always liking it.

Despite the challenges, looking after them has become such a reflex that I don't know what I'll do when they're older and more independent. My life's mission since these little people arrived has been attending to their every single need. Then all of a sudden, they go off on their own and don't need me to brush their teeth or wipe their noses? They won't be there asking me to help with every little thing? 'I'm hungry, dad. I'm thirsty, dad. Help me with this toy, dad. Daddy, I just go poos!' It's going to be a shock. As much as I complain about how needy they are; I'm missing them already. It's bizarre … the passage of time with children.

I suspect that when the kids leave it'll feel like the rug is being pulled out from under me. Yes, it's called empty nest syndrome and I'm afraid of it. That's why I really, really want to make the most of the time I do have with my little bubbies. That's the challenge; have more fun with them and do less griping and grumping. Focus on creating memories; not on the dried-out food that's always under the table. It's such a paradox; they drive you mad, but you love them so much.

Part of my empty nest fears are about losing control. These little representatives of me will be out in the world unmonitored, doing whatever they want, and I won't be by their side to direct and/or correct them. Yes, that's more the negative side of parenting but it still swims around in my head, right or wrong. They will express opinions to others without me to nudge them or take them aside and explain that it isn't wise to let everyone know what they're thinking. I know that sounds super-controlling and maybe a bit nuts; but can't I be honest here?

Yes; they'll move out and go to college and then have their first jobs and apartments, etc. I'll be at home with oodles of free time, wondering what they're up to. I'll text them each morning and they will probably look at their phones and think, 'what does he want now!' I'll just want to know that they're alive. And also, that they locked the doors before going to bed, ate a proper meal, didn't leave food to harden on the dishes overnight, and checked under the sheets for spiders; stuff like that. Ok; I might be exaggerating a little bit.

Last Friday at the coffee shop, I asked the woman behind the register if the retirees are more chipper on Fridays, like the nine-to-fivers. She said they were, but not for the same reason. It wasn't an old reflex from their working days. She said that most of her elderly customers were excited on Fridays because they would be getting weekend visits from their adult children and grandkids, etc. Then it hit me; I saw myself as an old man waiting for the best part of the week; a visit from my girls!

Memory is different for everyone. My own childhood is a collection of images charged with

The Best Job I ever Had

emotions; some great and some not so great. Things that I don't recall are my parents doing loads of laundry, chopping vegetables, vacuuming, and washing dishes. The consistent completion of these tasks was utterly critical to keep me alive, yet I remember none of it. These are the very same tedious chores that are doing me in as a SAHP ... and not surprisingly, what I grump about the most.

Although my mental snapshot collection doesn't contain images of my parents slinging around the Hoover or scrubbing pots, it does contain the grump. I want my kids' psychic photo album to be filled with pictures of happiness; not a moody, sour dad. Among my joyful memories are the times when my parents gave me their undivided attention and hung out with me. Spending time with them is what I must focus on to fill their hippocampi with the good stuff; not the grump.

Oh; as an aside, I just looked up what area of the brain stores memories; hence the hippocampus reference. I wasn't trying to be fancy for the sake of it. Strangely enough, this brain organ sounds like some sort of a cartoon. Welcome to the Hippo Campus, a school for hippos! SAHP wackiness again ... moving along.

Once again, all I can do is practice being mindful of the fact that this won't last forever. I don't want to feel regret. Regret for not enjoying this time with my best buddies, regret for shouting at them for just being kids, regret for constantly griping about having to clean up after them and officiate Barbie battles, etc. So, that's the daily goal. I know I can do it. I know I can get the most out of this invaluable opportunity if I stay reflective, positive, and not sweat the little things.

So, how do we keep the little things from making us sweat and then grump? In the next chapter I'll share some tips on parent survival.

Hacks, Tips, etc.

This final chapter is a random hodgepodge of tips and observations that will be quite familiar to just about all moms and dads. However, it's nice to get a different angle on things or reaffirm that you're not the only one out there dealing with this stuff. Please forgive me if there are repeats from previous chapters in here but if there are, those are the ones doing my head in and thus bear repeating.

I'll start with the most consistently traumatic scenarios. These are the things that give me the cold sweats. These are the culprits of my acute PTPD (Post Traumatic Parenting Disorder). Yes; I've used that one quite a bit … sorry.

Grocery Store- Don't Do It!

NEVER, EVER, if at all avoidable, bring kids to the grocery store ... or any type of store, for that matter. The psychological trauma from worrying about them getting smashed into by other shoppers' carts, incessantly saying 'no' and putting all the food, gadgets, and toys they put into the cart back onto the shelves is horrific. I'd rather spend a month in a Gulag than unnecessarily bring children shopping. I'd rather stab myself in the eye (repeatedly) with a pencil than go through that. But ... occasionally it has to happen. Your best bet is to feed them savouries from the bakery section. No sugary foods. May the Force be with you.

Avoiding Cabin Fever

Get your little people out of the house on weekends; even if for just a short trip to ... oh, I'm such a hypocrite; to the grocery store. Ok, if you have multiple kids, just take the most hyper one and leave the other(s) with your spouse/partner if applicable. If you don't need anything, just go get some toilet paper or alcohol. Parents always need that stuff, right? I guess the onset of cabin fever depends on multiple variables such as the kids' ages, their temperaments, etc. All I know is that a pyjama and movie day almost always ends in hyperkinetic disaster for our family. Even taking them around the block on their bikes/scooters will damp down the energy and quell an uprising.

Excursion Preparation- Expect the Unexpected

Whenever leaving the house with children, ALWAYS bring snacks and water… ALWAYS! Once a kid decides that they are hungry/thirsty, their ability to endure hardship is zero. They will nag you into madness until you give them a granola bar and juice or whatever. Be prepared. Don't lose brain cells because you weren't ready. Don't take risks with this one. It should be a reflex to pack the car with snacks and water but don't let them see you do it. Otherwise, they'll ask for that stuff while you're backing out of the driveway.

A variation on the above- always take extra food and water on the school run but leave it in the car. I park and then meet my kids right outside their classrooms. There is a little playground outside, and they horse around with their friends for a bit afterwards. This is a great way to get in an afterschool activity if you don't have something else scheduled like dance, gymnastics, or karate, etc. However, if you feed and water them, they'll want to stay for hours which will cut into your late afternoon chores. Once they moan about being hungry or thirsty, you say it's in the car and then off you go without any issues … mostly.

Anticipating Needs

Earlier I mentioned that a kid's ability to endure hardship is non-existent. This applies to everything; not just food. Once a need arises, if it isn't fulfilled NOW, they will make you pay. Yes; it's a good idea, in theory, to teach them to wait for things; to have patience. However, when you're trying to focus on other tasks, and they start bombarding you with 'right now's' it's futile to tell them to wait. They just keep hitting that button over and over. It's kind of like when adults want the elevator or traffic light to produce immediate results … they too, keep pressing the button.

Have colouring books, blank paper and crayons … anything to occupy them, when bringing the other kids to sports practice, dance class, etc. We've got a thirty-minute dance class for Emily right after school and because it's so short and she's only five, I stay until it's over. But four-year-old Zoe needs something to keep her busy for that half hour or it could get ugly. I bring her favourite toys or colouring-in stuff and sit on the floor with her. Beth is old enough to occupy herself.

Make sure they pee/poo before going out anywhere; even if you have to hold your kid over the toilet and squeeze them until it comes out. Yes; they will eventually have to use a public toilet but why go through this more often than necessary. Ask them if they have to use the bathroom thirty minutes before you go out. Then ask them again every ten minutes until you get results. Getting peed on in a public bathroom is no fun. Worrying about public bathroom germs is no fun. Sick kids are no fun.

As far as dinnertime goes; make sure you give them three of everything and tons of ketchup. That means three cups of water, three forks, three spoons, three knives, and three napkins. Ok, I'm exaggerating slightly; but only slightly. There's still no guarantee that you'll be able to have two consecutive bites of food, but it's worth a try.

Shopping with Multiple Children

If your kids are close in age and they're always fighting over toys, encourage them to pick the exact same Barbie (or whatever) when shopping. Sometimes on weekends, if we have the money and we're really exhausted and need something to occupy them, we'll buy some cheap toys. However, although you must let them choose what they want, try and steer the decisions so that they all end up with the same thing. Why? If different items are selected, by the time you get home they will want each other's toys and battles will ensue; thus ruining your peaceful afternoon.

Bribery- Do It!

Under extenuating circumstances, use chocolate to bribe your kids. If they are really, really driving you nuts and you have no energy for disciplining, use this technique to encourage good-ish behaviour or napping, etc. Show them the candy so they know how much there is available. This is important. Visuals are powerful. You and your spouse/partner will eat the majority of it but if the children see a lot, they will be more agreeable.

Gold stars are another great way to motivate them to behave. Of course, it depends on their age, but I've found it effective with Emily and Zoe. Verbal gold stars can work if you don't have stickers on-hand. If you say they'll get a gold star for brushing their teeth or getting dressed, they will usually comply. Grant the gold star in a praising tone and add one or two to make them extra happy. 'Three gold stars for brushing your teeth, Emily!' However, an actual gold star from a sticker pad is understandably more potent.

Don't let them see the entire pad of gold stars, though. Just stick a couple to your hand and walk into the room and show them. Like magic; those teeth are brushed, or they'll dress themselves without complaint. Ok; this works most of the time. If you need the big guns, just bring out the whole sticker pad and give them five each or something like that. The effectiveness will likely wane from there but if you're desperate for results, that'll work. You can also swap out gold stars for those cartoon Band Aids. I use the Peppa Pig and Minion ones. If possible, alternate gold stars and Band Aids to maintain your bargaining power.

I don't like bribing my kids but being in the trenches is different than discussing child-rearing while drinking tea and they're all napping or playing peacefully. When you are at your wits' end, sometimes bribery is the only viable option.

The NO! Button

I highly recommend getting yourself a NO Button. Kids ask for stuff incessantly and it's maddening. But to be fair, they either can't do most of these things for themselves or aren't allowed to. 'Oh, you want to pour the milk yourself, Johnny?' Not a chance in Hell, kid ... I'm not cleaning the floor again. So, children pretty much hear no (no! nope! forget it! when pigs fly! when you're eighteen!) all day long. Yes, I'm aware of the negative impact of the word no, but let's pretend this is the 1950's.

When you get tired of saying no to your kid (usually seven o'clock in the morning for me), just grab the NO Button and point it at the child. Before pressing the button, inhale the power of this wonderous device. Half the fun is pre-press. Then let them ask you yet again for candy or whatever and let em' have it ... NOOOO! The NO Button speaks for you and repeated pressing delivers the message about ten different ways. However, under no circumstances should you allow the child to press the button.

When they first hear the NO Button, their reaction will likely be a mixture of confusion, anger, and then desire ... to try this 'toy'. It's not their toy though, it's YOUR toy. If the child is allowed to press the NO Button, it's effectiveness will be diminished by at least seventy five percent and you'll have to put it away for a month. Once the child forgets about it, the device will return to roughly eighty percent power, but you'll never get it back to one hundred percent if they're allowed to press it even once.

I have two NO Buttons. One is the full-sized version and the other is a keychain model which seems ideal for the school run or grocery store, but it's not. It has a design flaw in that any sort of pressure will trigger a volley of No's. Too many times while digging in my pocket for a bankcard, I've heard a muffled electronic voice from my jeans ... NO! It's weird, so I don't recommend this model. It's like a talking pony that creepily neighs from the bottom of the toybox at three o'clock in the morning. Stick with the desktop NO Button but keep it up high or hidden behind the brown rice in the pantry.

Do you see how thorough my analysis of the NO Button was? That's what being a SAHP does to your brain. FYI- during the revision process, I cut two additional paragraphs about the NO Button because that would have been over the top. Crazy, huh?

The Family Taxi

From a parenting perspective, I cannot stress how monumentally important it is to keep your car in tip-top condition. It's a safety thing, but it's also a mental health thing. Without a car, you can't drop your kids off at school or day care. Think about that. It's disconcerting, isn't it?

Depending on your geographic situation, a vehicle that's out of commission could mean complete and total isolation. Minus the children, that could work out nicely. However, throwing them off their routine and being housebound is very combustible.

Even if your car is in perfect condition, make sure your bundles of joy don't leave the lights on and drain your battery. Surely, you've gotten frustrated with their hyper energy and just shooed them outside. Out! Out! Out! They can take that screaming outside so the neighbours can deal with it for a while. After all, it takes a village to raise a child, right? Truth be told, the neighbours on both sides of our house have sold within the last four months. Never found out why.

Anyway; back to that car battery. Zoe loves to play in the family truckster when ejected from the house. It's ok because the way our place is set up, you can see the car from the living room window. She messes with everything; and I mean everything. All of the switches, mirrors, vents, lights, etc. She has lots of fun playing race car driver. The biggest issue is the lights. During the day, it's hard to notice if they're on and we close the curtains before dusk.

I've had to ask neighbours for a jump on several occasions. These were the ones diagonally across the street and fairly out of earshot. They only hear the yelling and/or crying from the car as we come and go, versus the incessant chaos the closest neighbours are subjected to. In any event, keep an eye on the headlights and the internal lights as leaving them on overnight could mean you're screwed when it's time to do the school run.

Aside from being a kid and grocery shuttle, your car is a mobile trash can and toy box. It's also a boxing ring. Ok; more like a slapping and scratching ring. Where is a parent completely unable (not unwilling; that's different) to intercede during fights and mess-making? I know it's happening, but I must keep my eyes on the road. The kids know it and take maximum advantage!

I saw this video online where a dad makes these plexiglass dividers between his three little ones' car seats. It was brilliant. They can't slap/scratch each other or take toys, food, and those strangely precious scraps of paper away from each other. The other option is installing one of those button-operated glass limousine dividers. When a melee breaks out, just hit the button and drive on in peace.

Regrettably, I'm too tired to investigate either solution.

I never have time to thoroughly clean the car after a school run but do try to throw out stuff like half-eaten fruit and sandwiches as those things rot and bring vermin. Rats, mice, and roaches can cause pandemonium on the expressway if the children see or feel them scurrying about and you're focused on the road. Ok; my car isn't that bad, but it could easily get that way. Once the smell is unbearable, we do a big clean on the weekend. As you could imagine; the toys, apple cores, and little snack wrappers immediately begin accumulating again.

Go the Fu*k To Sleep! –
Part 2

Where do they get all of that energy from? No nap, check. Lots of exercise, check. Big, heavy meals, check. How is it that they are still bouncing off the walls at nine o'clock? One of the moms at school said they can tap into our energy. That's her theory as to why children often become preternaturally whizzed up just as we hit the wall and are about to collapse. Hmm ... this explains a lot. Because we are genetically and emotionally connected to our kids, they have access to our life force. Whoa!

This isn't really a hack ... it's the ultimate parent rant. What can we do but hope today is the day our kids just go to sleep when we announce that it's bedtime? I'd go right to sleep; wouldn't you? What's wrong with these little people? Yes; I've already covered this issue but since then, they've driven us over the edge innumerable times. I must elaborate further. And by the way; regardless of age, a kid can nap. Don't pay attention to those studies suggesting that children do not need naps after a certain age ... that's bullsh*t.

When we're on long weekend rides in the car, one of us is in charge of 'nap-patrol'. There's no way we are going to let a child sleep in the car and sabotage mom and dad's afternoon snooze ... not a chance. We play music that is not soothing, we sing our own off-key songs, and we employ the kids who aren't on the verge of nodding off to keep sleepyhead awake. We pay in chocolate and extra screen time. But seriously, weekends are tough on parents, we need that nap, right? I wonder how the ancients handled things; not just at bed/naptime, but all parenting challenges? That's certainly a question for the ages.

Now I must go and cut up some fruit and wipe a bum. Thanks a million for taking the time to read this story. I've only been at it a year and (of course) have so much more to learn about being a SAHP, and a parent in general. It has certainly been difficult, but I have no desire to return to office work. Paradoxically, this role has taken me longer to settle into than any other, but it's the best job I've ever had. I'll keep taking it one day at a time; chugging that coffee and hugging my kids.

*Oh; if you enjoyed this book, then I'd like to ask a favour. Would you be kind enough to leave a review on Amazon? This would mean the world to me as feedback completes the circle between writers and readers. I would greatly appreciate it. Just a short one is fine, and it doesn't have to be anything fancy. You rock!

Printed in Great Britain
by Amazon